PRACTICAL WORD POWER:
Dictionary-Based Skills in Pronunciation and Vocabulary Development

(An ESL Tutor's Script and Workbook)

by Richard Cavalier

Editor and Consultant
Dr. John Haskell

Authors Choice Press
San Jose   New York   Lincoln   Shanghai

Practical Word Power

Authors Choice Press
an imprint of iUniverse.com, Inc.

For information address:
iUniverse.com, Inc.
5220 S 16th, Ste. 200
Lincoln, NE 68512
www.iuniverse.com

Originally published by Delta Systems Co., Inc.

ISBN: 0-595-13048-8

Printed in the United States of America

To my five
foreign-born
grandparents

Acknowledgments: Many professionals and community groups have encouraged and supported the development and refinement of this book and the course it engenders in ESL (English as a Second Language).

The Chicago Urban Skills Institute at Harry S. Truman College (one of the City Colleges of Chicago) located in the Uptown community, provided the classroom base for the development of a course that would do what no other known course was capable of doing: providing quick mastery of pronunciation for groups of non-native speakers. Dr. Peyton S. Hutchi son awarded a Certificate of Recognition in 1981.

More than a hundred students were ultimately tutored over a period of several years. Among them were ABE, ACE, GED, and college-credit students, often mixed in the same class—and it worked. Without their enthusiasm for the results of the emerging course, it would not have been formalized.

During the long period of design and development, the program had the full support of Truman College President Dr. Wallace B. Appelson and his then-Director of Planning, Research, and Evaluation, Dr. Thomas W. Ryba, who sought funding for a tutor-orientation center at Truman. Dr. Jane Browne permitted a test with ACE students even though the class did not qualify (at only half the State's stipulated group size) for reimbursement. Dr. William Levin found meeting space for the groups when there was no room in the inn.

Aurora de la Torre, a teacher and ESL Coordinator at Truman, was instrumental in assembling classes. Her perfect bilingual skills were both an incentive and challege to students. Jeffrey P. Bright, Curriculum Specialist at CUSI, validated the program for broader adoption. Helius (Elio) DeArruda, then Chicago Coordinator for the Northern Area Adult Education Service Center, has assisted me in placing the project within the general context of local programs.

More recently, Fred Phillips, Instructor/Coordinator for the CCC Drop-In Literacy program at Robert Taylor Homes, in Chicago, arranged for me to tutor several of his charges. Kathy N., then reading at a high-fifth/low-sixth grade level, became the first native-speaker to complete the course, determined to outpace her daughters.

In Uptown Chicago, the Chinese Mutual Aid Association conducted the first test in an ethnic alternative school, tutored by Barbara Morton, a corporate librarian. Cha-Hee Stanfield, head of Bezazian branch library will host Uptown's first PWP orientation session for tutors from ethnic providers of social services.

Over a period of years, the Board and staff of the Uptown Chicago Commission supported the project by purchasing "loaner" dictionaries for my classes and also by seeking funding for a broad field implementation among ethnic organizations. This project was voted a priority item in the program goals of the organization.

To all, my thanks.

Finally, I owe more than thanks to ESL specialist Dr. John Haskell, Professor of Linguistics at Northeastern Illinois University, who has been reviewing and aiding since the first outline was committed to paper early in 1981. His patient (and occasionally impatient) criticisms and perceptive suggestions have resulted in a practical course for layman tutors in which professionals can recognize standard methodology, even though simplified. His editing and consulting expertise has given me the confidence to proceed into print with a program begun as a simple volunteer effort in the community.

ABOUT THE AUTHOR

Richard Cavalier is a consultant in group communications—meetings, training, and audiovisual presentations. He has published numerous articles in the trade press on the importance of identifying and protecting the message in business communications; and methodology from his two books on meeting management has been adopted as a standard by Meeting Planners International, the largest professional organization in that field.

He has traveled in more than forty countries—usually language handicapped—including over a year's stay in the Orient on military duty. Having studied academic German, Berlitz Spanish, and tutored French, and having memorized survival phrases in the Japanese and Korean languages (mutilating all without favoritism), Cavalier has learned *what works and why* in practical approaches to any foreign language.

His hometown in northern Minnesota was a turn-of-the-century center for immigrant labor. Because his grandparents' generation was predominently foreign-born, broken English was their norm. Standard American-English pronunciation was taught to young people in school, but the oldsters (apart from the rudiments of citizenship classes) were left to pick up English as best they could. Some did well—especially those who could learn from their children; others were locked out of main-stream activities permanently.

Cavalier has grown up witnessing the frustration, embarrassment, social strictures, and waste of human potentials derived from significant language handicaps. This book, based on years of his volunteer classroom tutoring, is his attempt to help people who want to help themselves.

TABLE OF CONTENTS

EDITOR'S INTRODUCTION

A few years ago I volunteered to make recordings for the blind. I did so under the mistaken impression that while I was doing a service, I would also be able to do some reading for my own pleasure. That was my first mistake, for as Don Knapp has frequently pointed out to us, reading aloud aborts the reading act and obliterates anything but occasional surface comprehension.

My second mistake was in thinking, somewhat naively, again, that my vocabulary was sufficiently large enough to make me capable of reading almost anything cold. I was, after all, a professor of linguistics, graduated from the University of Michigan and Columbia University, and, at that time, a teacher of English, history, and ESL for nearly twenty years. Imagine my chagrin to come acropper of words which I knew and used fully well, because I had failed to account for the difference in what I could read and use in writing and what I had never used orally and probably had never heard (or at least paid attention to) when used by others.

The words "hegemony," "scion," and "flaccid," come immediately to mind. I was reading, of all improbable things, Tolkien's essays on Beowulf. My monitor stopped me after my "treatment" of each of these words, referring me to the dictionary's rendering of the "correct" pronunciation. It was a humbling lesson to learn. It has, also, bothered me ever since. Not only the lack of my own dictionary knowledge, but to some extent the tyranny of the dictionary (that is, how it occasionally conflicts with spoken reality). I suppose that the pronunciation of "flaccid" is the best example. The dictionary uses the standard "ks" pronunciation for the "cc" as in "access" and "succeed," while I have never met anyone who didn't pronounce it with only an "s". More critical are such differences in the pronunciation of words like "metal" and "butter," where American speakers produce a sound closer to the "d" than the "t" the dictionary tells us is "correct."

I suppose that the last thing most native speakers, even educators, do when they come across a new or unfamiliar word or use of a word, is to look it up in the dictionary. First we skip it, hoping it won't affect our understanding. We will, if necessary, guess from the context or look for the writer's clues as to what is meant. If the word persists and resists these tactics, rather than looking for the dictionary, which is lying somewhere around the house, our next effort is usually to ask someone. Only as a last resort, and in desperation, do we get up from our chair or desk and search for the dictionary. We look up the pronunciation only when there is a conflict (or an embarassment) which we need to resolve.

Why are we so dictionary shy? It can't be simply laziness. Often, I would guess, it is because we really don't know how to use a dictionary efficiently. We have strange notions of what it contains. Also, a word is often followed by little more than a minimal definition—all too often one which is vague or abstract or as obtuse as the word we are attempting to identify.

Second language learners are more quick to use a dictionary, especially a bilingual one, than a native speaker. But they have little more knowledge than the native speaker has of how to use a dictionary beyond the same fumbling with inexact translations of words and the puzzling over which of the many possible definitions works for the context from which they are searching.

Certainly one of the last things that a dictionary user is really comfortable with is the Pronunciation Key—that list of symbols, diacritical marks and ligatures (which unfortunately each dictionary maker invents especially for their dictionary), which is meant to help the uninstructed reader to pronounce correctly those words with which they are unfamiliar.

In ESL, literacy, and bilingual-bicultural programs, the teaching of pronunci-ation has been incorporated, by and large, into the more important listening-speaking-grammar courses which tend to try to do everything for the learner, teaching them the whole language rather than segmenting or compartmentalizing it.

And yet one of the areas that gets short shrift is pronunciation, both of sounds and also of prosodic features such as stress, rhythm and intonation. It is the first area to fossilize, the first for both teacher and learner to overlook in the morass of syntax, vocabulary, and composition skills, which seem more important to learn.

We have, often, all but admitted that although we have the obligation and the duty to teach students the sounds of English that are new to them (or are causing difficulty with articulation) what we cannot do is insure that they will continue to pronounce English correctly after they have been taught a basic vocabulary. Part of the problem is the rapid introduction to, and large volume of, vocabulary that the new language learner is put into contact with both orally and more particularly in writing. How do the students, short of asking, learn to say new words? How can they improve their current pronunciation? Even better, how can they acquire skills which will sustain them in the acquisition of additional vocabulary as they progress in the language? Surely one possibility is being able to use an American English dictionary (or any dictionary) effectively.

One of the many things a dictionary does is to indicate how a word is pronounced in standard American English, including the alternate (although still standard) forms which might be heard from various speakers. It seems logical that if one could teach a student how to use the Pronunciation Key to a dictionary effectively, it would help the student produce better pronunciation *and* master a skill that will not disappear when the teacher does.

Richard Cavalier's training program, *Practical Word Power* (*PWP*), which appears in this volume, does just that. In a short, intensive set of six to eight training sessions, *PWP* provides an introduction to American English pronunci-ation via those symbols used in the dictionary. In this case, the American Heritage (Dell paperback Second College Edition) Dictionary is used; but certainly, the *PWP* program is easily adaptable to any American dictionary. *PWP* also reinforces the use of these symbols through simple, practical exercises.

A linguist, looking at the Key to Pronunciation in any dictionary, blanches at the disparity between phonology and the way the dictionary describes our English system. Most linguists, for example, would consider the "a" in father and the "o" in pot to be similar if not the same sound, or the "ur" of urge, the "er" of butter to be different only in stress. But linguists are not all that consistant in their use of symbols, either (note, for example, the different systems used by Pike versus Trager, and Smith versus IPA, etc.) These conflicts and confusions can overwhelm the unprepared student.

More needs to be learned than the symbols, the diacritical marks (tents, arcs, dots, bars, etc.) and the doubled letters (ligatures) used to reprint such sounds as "th" and "sh". All dictionaries provide generally good information about stress, dictionary ligatures, vowels with "r," syllabic consonants, etc.—information which most dictionary users never read.

This training course will help the students to recognize these symbols, to understand them, to put them to use in improving their ability to pronounce standard American English.

This book may seem at times to defy the "rules" of language, and it leaves out a lot of peripheral things a pronunciation text or teacher might by training provide. For instance, PWP does not deal with articulation, per se, though there is some information and a few exercises for certain sounds in the appendix. A person giving this training course may wish to consult someone who has specialized training in the teaching of pronunciation if problems persist for some students; and the book itself indicates decision points and criteria to be considered. *PWP* does not claim to improve English grammar directly; yet it contributes to learning and the motivation to learn.

PWP is not a linguistics course, but it does very well what it sets out to do: introduce that narrower skill of using the dictionary key to pronunciation—*and it does so in an original way*. It provides access to a different approach to teaching pronunciation which any instructor or student can follow. Any caring person who is willing and able to read through this text (plus a dictionary Pronunciation Key and explanatory notes) will be able to help almost any student pronounce English words better and learn to use the dictionary as a means of continuing to pronounce words better. I cannot imagine a more straight-forward training program. It can give any student *permanent* access to standard American English pronunciation. I think you will find it a useful course for your second language students.

John F. Haskell
Chicago
October, 1988

AUTHOR'S FORWARD

Everyone needs the dictionary to verify pronunciation and spelling, apart from getting definitions. Curiously, these key dictionary skills are rarely taught below college level, and then essentially to theatre and education majors.

This book and course were created for the express purpose of simplifying (and so, encouraging) the teaching/learning of standard American-English pronunciation using dictionary diacritical codes. Its content and structure were developed and refined in the classrooms of Truman College (one of the City Colleges of Chicago), in the Uptown community of Chicago. Uptown is a magnet for immigrant and refugee populations in the Midwest, and Truman College has the largest concentration of non-native students in the city and state, offering one of the nation's broadest programs targeting this special population.

In addition to its proved usefulness with adult non-native speakers, a number of professionals have suggested that the book and course also seem appropriate for Americans who speak—and wish to change—non-standard dialects. The preliminary trials indicate that it will work for native speakers with only minor adjustments, already outlined in the text.

Several things are unique with this book. First, it permits volunteers to tutor standard pronunciation and related conversational English skills even without prior teaching experience or professional background in linguistics. Second, it permits those volunteers to tutor groups of up to ten students, although one-to-one arrangements are still prevalent in volunteer networks. Third, the course teaches the pronunciation skills comprehensively, so no further classroom work is needed: the student is self-sufficient in vocabulary development ever after. That promotes self-confidence and self-reliance. Fourth, its whole-language approach to the pronunciation focus allows it to hone related skills in conversation, leading to improved comprehension and fluency, as well.

As a result, employers, ethnic and religious organizations, public agencies, unions, and even concerned individuals can take direct action in an area previously considered prohibitively complex for non-professionals. Moreover by orienting tutors as well as by tutoring students, community colleges can multiply the effects and benefits of existing budgets and resources.

There is abundant need for a quantum growth in capability. Although numerous literacy organizations are already functioning across the country, all the efforts of educational systems and volunteer networks *together* are now reaching about ten percent of the estimated need, according to reports quoted by the Business Council for Effective Literacy.

Because the Federal government (and therefore most states and interested foundations) has funded only basic levels of reading/writing—that is, through Grade 5.9, or fifth grade completed—inadequacy is built into the present system. Guidelines for the Amnesty program have not been announced as of press time.

Consequently, those who attain a sixth grade level or more often must attend formal classes at their own expense or remain forever at marginal levels of competency. Since many persons with marginal communication skills are already working long hours at low-paying jobs *because of language handicaps*, formal classes are not a realistic alternative.

Traditional policies and approaches are being reassessed at many levels at present. New approaches are certain to result.

Meanwhile, in its own area of delivering pronunciation skills—and so, self-sufficiency in vocabulary development—*Practical Word Power* is a proved alternative that can make a difference...now!

Richard Cavalier

PREFACE

ABOUT THIS BOOK AND COURSE

The central skill taught to adult students in this program is the mastery of a dictionary pronunciation key, with its diacritical code marks, so that students can: a) develop vocabulary as needed, independently of further classroom supervision; b) improve conversational ability and comprehension by pronouncing English words recognizably, with an accuracy of acceptable to perfect; c) recognize spoken words not now associated with known spellings of their reading vocabulary; and d) increase their self-reliance and so their confidence in speaking English. That, in turn, will increase their effectiveness as neighbors, employees, and fellow citizens.

You, as a tutor, can help them reach that goal.

This book has been created as a tutor's script and training guide for adults. Even a tutor who has never before "taught" any individuals or groups can teach this course. *Practical Word Power* makes that possible by presenting all necessary "technical" background information as verbatim explanation—an established training technique. You simply read the script aloud and then do the blackboard work and exercises it clearly outlines. If you have ever been involved in a Scout troupe activity or little league sports team, you will find the adults far easier to deal with!

Although this course can work with only one or two students, it was designed to tutor up to ten in the same group. The presentation material is identical regardless of the size of the class. Only the recitation time varies with the number of students, and the workbook material makes allowances for these variations.

When tutoring your class, you can concentrate on the practical examples, not theory, because the examples are based on relevant educational principles. As a tutor, you will be sharing your understanding of your native language; you will not be making speeches as an "educator." Yet, despite this unpretentious approach, you will be helping your students change and enhance their lives, by gaining a pivotal skill in self-improvement and self-reliance.

This program was developed over a period of several years while the author worked with more than a hundred students representing all language groups. They were involved variously in General Education Diploma (GED), Adult Basic Education (ABE), Adult Continuing Education (ACE), and college-degree programs...randomly mixed in the same class.

That total exposure to the real-life needs of students at all levels of education and virtually all backgrounds has affected both the content and structure of this book and its program.

Flexible Structure:

The drills and the exercises emphasize the interests, and the areas of most frequent difficulty, expressed or noted in the classes. Everything scripted has a purpose, and tutors should not arbitrarily eliminate topics. Within those topics, tutors can allow more or less time according to the response of the students. Basic time allowances are suggested throughout. So even though the course material is carefully set out, you have a great deal of flexibility in dealing with the needs of any given group.

Focus:

Similarly, the structure of the book and course focuses on the practical application of discussion and drill work to the learning of the dictionary code and the mastery of pronunciation and phrasing. We avoid teaching rules, for the most part, because rules have exceptions which must also be taught. Ultimately it's more useful to note that there are no firm rules. That reinforces student dependence on dictionary entries, rather than guesswork.

Does it work? Remarkably well!

Students in the developmental classes ranged from low-fluency with high native-language education to high-fluency (heavily accented) with low native-language education—and all points between. Not all students finished the program, of course, but of those who did, all had mastered the dictionary code system, with dramatic improvement in oral communication.

Specifically, students will be able, after just eight sessions, to open the dictionary to a random page and pronounce the longest word on that page— acceptably to perfectly (see the section "A Word about Perfection"). Individual performance on three random selections proves the ability to the student and peers.

Exercises stressing reading interpretation and phrasing-for-sense help to move the course skills beyond simply word sounds. If you choose to include job-related vocabulary, you'll find options for structuring already set out.

When we consider the benefits of clear speech to the student and to his or her associates on the job, in the community, in stores and offices which are a part of everyone's daily routine, then we understand why, if the potential of any individual is lost because of a language barrier, we are all losers. This book can help create the skills that enable all of us to win!

HOW TO USE THIS WORKBOOK

Self-Help Structure:
This book contains all the information and technical background information you will need to tutor this pronunciation and vocabulary development course
in English as a Second Language (ESL). Some of the course material is presented
as verbatim script: read it aloud just as it appears. Other material is intended for
blackboards or handouts or discussion—all stipulated. Every task or
demonstration is clearly indicated, along with guidelines, if those are appropriate.
Incidental information (neither read aloud or "done" as a task) is presented as
notes to you. All are carefully sorted out. For instance:

> TUTOR: Read aloud to your students all the
> discussion and general information that appears in this
> format on all right-hand (odd-numbered) pages
> throughout the lesson pages of this book.
> All necessary explanations of linguistic information
> and dictionary diacritical codes are presented in this
> way. You do not need to "create" basic explanations.

**NOW DO THE STIPULATED TASK OUTLINED
IN LARGE CAPITAL LETTERS ON ALL LEFT
HAND (EVEN NUMBERED) PAGES.** SMALL
CAPITALS INDICATE ADDITIONAL INFORMATION TO
GUIDE YOU IN CARRYING OUT THE TASK.
    DO NOT READ THIS MATERIAL ALOUD! RATHER,
PRESENT THE BLACKBOARD OR PRINTED MATERIALS
AND/OR CONDUCT THE ORAL DRILLS, ETC., EXACTLY
HOW AND WHEN THEY APPEAR IN THE TEXT.

BLACKBOARD MATERIALS ARE BOXED, LIKE THIS,
SO YOU ARE ALERTED BY VISUAL CUE. THE WORD
"PRINT" APPEARS FOR REINFORCEMENT.
OBVIOUSLY "PRINT" IS NOT PART OF THE MATERIAL
THAT ACTUALLY APPEARS ON THE BLACKBOARD. IN
THE SAME WAY, THE WORD "ADD" INDICATES THAT
THE ADDITIONAL BLACKBOARD MATERIAL IS PART
OF THE PRECEDING CHAIN OF THOUGHT.

    NOTE: Special information regarding options or other
decisions or presenting technical information to you alone
(such as articulation of sounds or a point of grammar,
etc.,) appears like this, also on the left-hand page. Read
and know before class, because references to Appendix
material presented here will help you to be best prepared.

Advance Preparation:

As you prepare for your very first class, read this entire book, cover to cover. That umbrella understanding will help you to fit all the pieces of the eight sessions into the proper pattern. Any dictionary you happen to have at hand will be suitable for the initial reading, as long as you understand that the markings of diacritical codes will not match what you see in this book, unless you have the recommended dictionary.

After the initial reading, and before you begin to prepare the details of the First Session, buy the recommended dictionary (or decide whether you wish to change each and every blackboard example throughout the course). Read its introductory information—there's a wealth of course-related knowledge there.

Then, with the classroom dictionary text in hand, re-read the First Session, decide how you will handle handout or blackboard work, etc., and make notes to yourself on the pages, if you like. Allow a couple of hours, so that you can think your way through the class.

Visual Consistency

You might notice that certain letters of the alphabet appear either in upper case (capitals) or lower case in the script. To minimize the possibility of misreading, single letters are shown in upper case, and letters in pairs or series are shown in lower case. Similarly, in blackboard matter, single-letter captions will be capitalized, and all dictionary-related entries will be lower case.

In theory that sounds fine; in practice it occasionally looks strange. Yet is seems to serve the purpose of distinguishing among entries. Content is not affected; so please indulge our purpose.

Content and Timing:

All classes are designed to be completed within two hours each. To allow for variations in time resulting from classes of different sizes, you can vary the amount of time spent on particular items. In any case, do not belabor any item on which the class performs satisfactorily. . .move on and use that time on problem situations, if any, or on practice drills.

Because content and structure reflect actual classroom experience, please do not make arbitrary changes. For instance, we recommend that all these sessions be delivered in two-hour blocks, not less frequently than once a week, nor more frequently than twice weekly. The long time blocks aid the wholistic sense of what's happening, and also eliminate the need for extra review sessions.

In employment situations, the only time available might be the lunch hour. In that case, halving the sessions might be the only alternative to not conducting them at all. A break-point is indicated clearly in the First Session if it is unavoidable. Half-way points are easily calculated for other sessions.

For your first eight-session course or two, follow the book closely. At that time, you will be familiar enough with the operation of the course to make adjustments based on student need. Yet, do not *eliminate* any topics!

And if you're feeling a little timid the first time out, schedule only four or six students. More free time will contribute to a more informal feeling. But remember that you are simply presenting the fine points of your own language, which you use every day. With this book, you become an expert in pronunciation. It's challenging, but not difficult. In fact, you'll probably amaze yourself!

ADDITIONAL RESOURCES

Besides this book you will need other materials, from time to time, in order to conduct the practical exercises for the class. These include:

a) *several paper-back, pocket-size dictionaries,* all of the kind you select as your course text. The "recommended" dictionary will be discussed in a following section. Provide "loaners" (at least one dictionary per pair of students) during each class period to avoid embarrassing those students who can't afford to buy a copy or who already own a different type.

b) *blackboard and chalk* (or felt pens and oversize chart paper sheets). In all eight sessions, you will be spelling and annotating problem words and examples.

c) several copies of *maps of the city and its public transportation system.* This practical exercise is optional, but especially helpful if students are having difficulty with city street and place names, or with transfers from transit route to other routes.

d) *handout copies of the Vocabulary Drill Charts* from this book, to be duplicated in the quantity needed.

e) several copies of the *entertainment section* of the local newspaper and/or nightlife guides of the type found in hotels.

Only one or two of these resource items will be used in any one session. You should determine that you are fully prepared for each class by reading quickly through the appropriate lesson pages an hour or so in advance of the class, even if you have previously "studied" the same material. Some of the exercises depend on the availability of the stipulated materials.

Because the First Session contains so much material that might be new to you as well as the students, it might take longer to prepare than will the subsequent sessions. Give it the time it needs, knowing the time requirement is not typical of the program as a whole.

Given the resource materials outlined, the course is ready to be implemented as it appears. Teachers and industrial trainers can orient tutors toward specific methods and tests, if consistency of tutoring style is desired, but the book is intended to be self-explanatory and self-help for the tutor. No formal tutor-training session is needed.

SELECTING PROSPECTIVE STUDENTS

As already stated, this program targets persons of middle competency levels in second-language English conversation and vocabulary development. Specific guidelines can be found in the Prerequisites section. Exceptions follow here.

Advanced students can benefit from this course if they are highly literate but retain an objectionable accent, or have never learned to pronounce via diacritical codes, or want to improve a rusty skill. Usually, at an advanced level, the students are prepared to proceed faster than this lesson plan provides. Accommodate them by telescoping exercises they have already mastered, and just proceed into the next session's material, if necessary.

However, because large variations in speaking skills would penalize any middle-level students in the same class, do not mix advanced- and middle-levels. Advanced students also tend to have more and different kinds of questions; so the class periods usually have a freer flow.

Follow their needs *after* presenting the basics of this text in each respective session. On the whole, it is best that a beginning tutor not take an advanced group until after successfully tutoring one or more classes for middle-level students. A good working knowledge of course content is the very best preparation for advanced groups.

Never attempt to teach this dictionary skills course to prospective students who have poor literacy skills in English and/or their native language. Illiterate and low-literacy groups often cannot comprehend the concepts of either dictionaries or diacritical codes, nor can they comprehend the level of discussion needed to succeed. If under-qualified individuals enter your class and fail, *the damage done to their self-confidence could be serious and lasting.*

American-born students have both a more fluent command of their English dialect than do non-native speakers and a totally different understanding of the language and their relationship to it. Therefore, although this course is appropriate for native-born speakers of non-standard dialects, do not mix them with non-native learners. Conduct separate courses; a slight text change is marked in the First Session.

Various language groups can be mixed in the same class to good effect. Although student abilities might vary widely within the middle range of skills, all are likely to be beginners with the diacritical codes. That alone is a leveler. Different ethnic backgrounds add interest to class discussions and help to assure all students that problems with English are universal, not theirs alone. This helps to produce a healthy motivation to work and master the course materials.

PREREQUISITES

THE TUTORS: All tutor candidates must speak/read/write a standard American-English; that is, speech and usage consistent with the language used on national radio and TV news broadcasts. Perfection of grammar or dulcet vocal tones are not the salient skills for tutors.

Anyone who can model the correct sounds as indicated by the dictionary diacritical marks for the given code words can be a competent tutor. This course was designed so that tutors do not need prior teaching experience.

For obvious reasons, it is preferable to use native-born Americans as tutors. Bilingual first-generation Americans can often deal especially effectively with non-native learners not highly schooled in their native language; but take care that occasional use of the native language does not dilute the benefits of this course.

If bilingual tutors are considered, they must be perfectly bilingual: that is, their English pronunciation must be dictionary-standard. BILINGUAL TUTORS WITH FOREIGN ACCENTS (NO MATTER HOW FLUENT IN SPEAKING) WILL TEACH DISTORTED SOUNDS THAT COULD PRODUCE A PERMANENT HANDICAP FOR SOME STUDENTS!

THE STUDENTS: All student candidates must have a middle-level competence in reading and/or conversational skills. Inadequate communications skills are normal and expected: improving those skills is one purpose of this course.

Persons highly educated in their native language can probably succeed at borderline, low-middle proficiency in English conversation if they have superior study skills. Persons of moderate- or low-level formal education in their own language should have middle or high-middle conversational skills before being admitted to this course.

It is impossible to define "middle" proficiency precisely. However, these benchmarks should help to identify candidates, whether or not they have already been "graded" by formal educational testing:
  a) late-fifth or early-sixth grade reading/vocabulary levels; or
  b) ESL levels III, IV, or V in any six or eight level system; or
  c) two years' academic study of English in their home country; or
  d) six to twelve months' active usage of English in daily life.

Any of these routes to proficiency is generally workable, since students do need reading skills at a level where dictionary usage can fairly be expected. DO NOT ALLOW UNQUALIFIED BEGINNERS TO ENTER THIS COURSE.

A WORD ABOUT "PERFECTION"

At about the mid-point of this course, the individual Performance Standard paragraphs in the lessons stipulate that you should "work toward perfection" of the sounds and words your students are producing.

Perfection as used in the course context should indicate your clear understanding of their spoken words, close to dictionary or broadcast standards, in all newly-learned vocabulary. Absolute perfection probably can never be achieved because a) several "standards" exists, which precludes purity; and b) "fossilized" incorrect pronunciation is difficult to overcome.

When referring to "standard" or "broadcast-standard" English we should all understand that both are generalizations geared to a broad norm. Not all announcers pronounce all words exactly alike. No two dictionaries show exactly the same pronunciation for all words; some words have two or more accepted pronunciations. Professional linguists argue constantly about the production of some sounds in some words. Distinct regional dialects are heard across the U.S., and each is "standard" within its geographical boundaries. British-, Canadian-, and Australian-English are also "standard" Englishes.

For practical purposes, then, "standard pronunciation" for this course means *standard to your dictionary textbook*. Expect and permit the same minor variations evident in the pronunciation patterns of you and your friends.

Clarity is salient. Sounds are "acceptable" when there is no confusion with similar sounds and words. When any student can accurately and consistently mimic the tutor *and can convert that accuracy to the Vocabulary Drill Chart and his dictionary tests*, that student has "perfected" those sounds...and has also achieved the goal this course sets for itself.

Consequently, the tutor *must* meet the *dictionary standard*.

As this course is structured, correctly-learned vocabulary soon dilutes the effect of fossilized pre-class vocabulary, creating rapid overall improvement. Also, problem word exercises in this text help to correct the most glaring errors *incidentally*—old vocabulary is NOT our focus. Given model dictionary sounds and their new learning, students can improve their own accents over time.

Fossilized mispronunciations are the result of perhaps years of habit—they will not disappear by magic. To concentrate on old vocabulary is virtually to preclude new learning; so we have chosen to be pro-active, not remedial.

So be generous in recognizing legitimate improvements your students make. Your encouragement and enthusiasm for their progress will accomplish more through motivation than will constant interruption to correct petty details. Strengthen their confidence in their ability to speak, and you will ensure ultimate fluency.

WHAT THIS WORKBOOK
AND SYSTEM CAN DO

When you use this program and system, you are providing a shortcut to the students' mastery of the dictionary pronunciation key, leading to their expanded working vocabularies. That, in turn, improves their speaking/reading comprehension through phrasing and interpretation exercises.

Practical Word Power is perhaps the first modular course to present pivotal pronunciation skills almost solely based on dictionary information—especially when intended to be tutored by volunteers.

It is often difficult for native-speakers to understand the importance of a program that seems so logical, for a number of reasons. First, most of us learn correct pronunciation by osmosis and constant input (modeling) from our parents, peers, and teachers over many years. Dictionary code usage is often taught to us incidentally, if at all, not as a formal sequence. Many people have problems with diacritical codes throughout their lives.

Second, few people are prepared to tutor others in pronunciation because both phonetics (the system of how to teach speech sounds) and phonics (the elementary schools system of teaching reading and pronunciation through phonetic interpretation) are rarely taught below the college level. As a result, most people feel insecure in a knowledge area that is quite simple to master.

Third, many students already use commercial bilingual dictionaries by foreign publishers. Some English sounds cannot be accurately rendered in print using foreign-language code combinations; and some dictionaries teach the British-English pronunciation, including such soft-R endings as mothah (mother), fathah (father), etc. Multiple codes used in a student group can produce conflicting pronunciation patterns that inhibit learning rather than aid it. Do not permit your students to use bilingual dictionaries from foreign publishers (except for translation purposes) until you have first verified their accuracy in relation to the course textbook.

Students who apply themselves can learn to reproduce all dictionary- or broadcast-standard American-English sounds acceptably within two or three sessions. Anyone who is free of physical speech impediments can achieve virtual perfection of individual sounds and drill words by the end of the fifth session. Subsequent sessions reinforce these skills and shift focus to interpretive functions and phrasing-for-sense. In the process, your role as tutor shifts from speaker/teacher to listener/coach; and the course becomes student-oriented. At that point, focus on their individual strengths and needs.

What your students will accomplish in only eight sessions (about two hours per session) will astound you. You will hear the sounds when they are ready to try their wings. Just nudge them and let them fly!

WHAT THIS WORKBOOK
AND SYSTEM CANNOT DO

Keep in mind that this course will achieve exactly what the program was designed to achieve. It cannot do things for which it was not designed. It does not provide remedial reading. It does not provide a comprehensive course in linguistics or grammar. It does not extinguish the faulty learning that has resulted in fossilized elements of incorrect pronunciation, although, as stated earlier, it can make a significant contribution toward the student awareness leading to correction.

Correct the serious mispronunciations of old vocabularies by example without making an issue of it. *Do not attempt to correct each and every mispronounced word from their old vocabularies.* If you fall into that trap, the class will quickly become bogged down in irrelevancies, and you will not convey the *ideas* and *concepts* which create the understand of the causes of mispronunciation. Once they understand the basic concept of pronunciation, students will be able to continue to improve their skills outside the class.

The only persistent problem for some students might be the trilled-R or the flap-R, both created with the tip of the tongue against the gum ridge. The formation of the sound of "R" is a reflex action used throughout their lifetimes. To change permanently to an American-R (the retroflex-R) is something that some of them will not accomplish in this course...and possibly never. If the word is clear, and if the student is making an effort to reproduce the American-R, his performance is satisfactory. You will find how-to information about the mechanics of reproducing the American-R (as well as other of the more difficult sounds) in the pertinent section of the First Session and also in Appendix A.

Any student who needs substantially more work in areas other than those provided in this course should be referred to appropriate courses in the school system.

CHOOSING THE DICTIONARY TEXTBOOK

In theory, any dictionary can be used as the basis for this program, and more than a dozen types are available in paperback alone. The problem, from the standpoint of the user, is that each publisher uses a different pronunciation key. Discrepancies among codes can create chaos in the preparation of classroom examples. Therefore, this course has of necessity selected one dictionary for teaching purposes.

The examples presented in this book are keyed toward *The American Heritage Dictionary*, based on the Houghton-Mifflin Second College Edition, 1983; published paperback by Dell Publishing Company. There are changes of pronunciation between Dell editions.

You may choose to adapt our examples to any other dictionary. If you adapt, be certain to verify and/or change every diacritical code marking throughout the program *prior* to beginning to instruct.

Despite the shortcoming of extremely small print the Dell dictionary offers two important advantages. First, it uses a short, simple pronunciation key, covering the most important sounds. Second, of all paperback dictionaries, only the Dell edition places the vowel code at the foot of each page for easy comparison. Such comparison is the crux of the skill of deciphering new-word sounds via the diacritical codes.

Extensive codes used by some paperbacks and most unabridged dictionaries present fifty or more vowel-sound symbols alone, plus consonants and ligatures. In the classroom, that means many additional units of information to be memorized and acted upon with *no* particular benefit. The extremely subtle differences in sounds identified by precision symbols can be of value to scholars but not to the everyday user. The ears of language-handicapped persons are not often attuned to subtle variations, and they should not be unnecessarily burdened.

If you do not have a specific reason for choosing another textbook, it is to your advantage to use the Dell edition mentioned above.

GRADING PERFORMANCE

If you are required to grade your students, you might wonder whether to use broad (satisfactory, inadequate, unsatisfactory) or narrow (letters or numbers) grading categories.

We recommend using a broad category for at least the first several sessions, switching to a narrow grading scale for the later sessions and the newspaper tests and final exam. That's a practical choice: to attempt to grade up to ten students on a specific scale covering about forty-five separate sounds would be maddening.

You might find it helpful to adapt the suggested basic registration and course grading form on page , if a specific grading form is not provided.

GETTING PERSONAL

For some students, you might be the only native-speaker with whom they feel comfortable talking. Therefore you might be asked for information or advice on topics not directly related to class.

Unless you are a professional in the subject matter of the question, a good rule of thumb is not to offer advice on any topic. Instead, refer the student to an appropriate professional within the school system.

Questions not directly related to the school system often relate to procedures with governmental agencies. If approached, you might provide the telephone numbers of the proper agency in writing, and it might be necessary for you to make a few phone calls in order to get those numbers. But let the students make their own appointments. One reminder inquiry from you a week or so later is helpful. It confirms both your personal interest and their need for self-help.

FINDING COURAGE

If you are new to tutoring, all of this might sound complex. It's not. Everything you need is in the dictionary and this book, augmented by the resource materials stipulated in the lesson plans.

Beyond that, what is required is a willingness to model for others the words and sounds of your own language. Don't sell yourself short. If you make an effort, you could grow along with your students.

Even if you can't work a miracle in only eight sessions, you certainly can give the miracle of hope a solid boost.

FIRST SESSION

FIRST SESSION

Notes:

Tasks:

DURING YOUR PRELIMINARY, PRE-CLASS STUDY OF THIS TUTORING SESSION, LIST MATERIALS NEEDED FOR THE CLASS HERE:

IN YOUR CLASSROOM, AT THE TIME OF THE FIRST SESSION, **PRINT YOUR NAME ON THE BLACKBOARD**, TOGETHER WITH YOUR TELEPHONE NUMBER IF YOU ARE WILLING TO BE REACHED. THEN, WHEN THE GROUP IS ASSEMBLED, BEGIN TO READ ALOUD:

NOW SAY THIS———▶

KEEPING RECORDS? PASS AROUND YOUR VERSION OF A SIGN-UP SHEET (OR USE THE ONE FOUND ON PAGE 247). START THE SHEET AROUND IN ONE DIRECTION AND **GET VERBAL IDENTIFICATION** IN THE OTHER.

NOW SAY THIS———▶

(next page)

F I R S T   S E S S I O N

◄——— *DURING ADVANCE PREPARATION, DO THIS*

(TO BEGIN INSTRUCTING CLASS, THE TUTOR SAYS:)

Hello. My name is _____. All of you have said you wish to improve your conversational skills by improving your pronunciation of American English. This course will help you to do that. If you listen and practice and apply the ideas we discuss here, then you will be able to pronounce new words almost perfectly...the very first time...using only a standard dictionary. Other benefits can include an increased vocabulary and improved comprehension when writing and speaking.

Would you like that? (GET A RESPONSE)

Do you believe it? (MOST DOUBT IT.)

Well, believe it. After just two class sessions, you will be able to repeat all the basic English sounds correctly. After three or four sessions you will hear yourself saying new words perfectly from the dictionary.

And by the last of the eight sessions, you will be able to use this dictionary so well that you can open it to any page and pronounce the longest word correctly. You will no longer need a tutor for pronunciation — you will be free to develop your own vocabulary as you need it.

Is that worth working for? (GET A RESPONSE.)

If you work at the ideas we discuss, you will progress very rapidly... I promise you.

Because the sound of your own native language will affect your ability to reproduce English sounds, I would like to take time to find out from each of you the name of the country you grew up in and the language you spoke at home. Also, I'll send this permanent class registration sheet around. Please print your name and the other information it asks for.

◄——— NOW DO THIS

Notes: Tasks:

IF YOU LIKE, REPEAT THEIR NAMES FOR ACCURACY, BUT BE AWARE
OF A SPECIAL "NAMES" EXERCISE IN THE FOURTH LESSON. **JUST
USE THIS OPPORTUNITY TO HEAR THE ACCENTS AND
ASSESS THE INDIVIDUAL PROBLEMS.** DON'T MEMORIZE
NAMES: THAT IS THE PURPOSE OF THE SIGN-UP SHEET. WHEN
ALL HAVE SPOKEN AND THE LIST IS IN HAND, CONTINUE:

NOW SAY THIS———▶

ON BLACKBOARD, PRINT:
cane/plain

NOW SAY THIS ———▶

PRINT:
plaid

NOW SAY THIS ———▶

PRINT:
said

NOW SAY THIS ———▶

PRINT:
maid

While the sheet is going around, each of you can tell the class your name, nationality, and how long you have been in the United States. We'll begin on this side...(INDICATE SOMEONE).
◄——— NOW DO THIS

UNDERSTANDING PROBLEM SOURCES

There are two main reasons why all foreign languages present problems to all adult learners. First, each language has sounds which are at least slightly different from those of the native language we learned by constant correction and imitation over many years. So, having an accent in a second language is normal. Most Americans think accents are charming *IF* the words are clear. Otherwise, accents are problems.

Second, the usual accent problem is made worse in the English language because English is a crazy language and because spelling and pronunciation in English are *not* always closely related. So, even native-born Americans must use the dictionary to confirm the pronunciation of unusual new words.

In English, different combinations of letters can have exactly the same sound. Also, the same combinations of letters can have different sounds, depending on the word itself, not on the surrounding letters in the word. It can be confusing until you know what to do about it: *check the dictionary!* Of course you could also ask a knowledgeable native speaker, but they are not always nearby when needed. Your best bet is to know how to use the dictionary.

Let me give you some examples of how irregular English is:
◄——— NOW DO THIS

Even though they are spelled differently, these two words, "cane" and "plain" have identical final sounds. That is, they *rhyme*.

Now, if I change the last letter of the word "plain," I form a new word with a new sound: Say "plain." (ALL REPEAT.)
◄——— NOW DO THIS

This word is "plaid," a pattern in cloth. Say "plaid" (ALL REPEAT.) But if I change the beginning letters and keep the ending, I get yet another new sound:
◄——— NOW DO THIS

You recognize this very common word, don't you? The word "said" is said a hundred times a day, and most non-native speakers say it *in*correctly. Repeat it correctly after me. Say "said" (ALL REPEAT)

Or, if I change the first letter again, this time to an "M", I get yet another pronunciation of the vowels.
◄——— NOW DO THIS

Say "maid" (ALL REPEAT)

Notes: Tasks:

THEN PRINT:
year/bear/early

NOW SAY THIS ──────▶

CIRCLE THE E-A-R PORTION
OF EACH WORD

PRINT:
though/through
enough/ought

PRINT:
pear/pair/pare

POINT TO THE CORRECT WORD AS YOU SAY IT IN THE SENTENCE.

PRINT:
to/too/two

POINT TO THE CORRECT WORD AS YOU SAY IT

◀——— NOW DO THIS

These words are pronounced "year," "bear," and "early"...three distinct results even though the three key letters (E-A-R) remain the same.

Say, "year, bear, and early." (ALL REPEAT. LISTEN AND REPEAT, IF NECESSARY.)

Here's another example. The same four letters (O-U-G-H) appear in all four words, but the sound is different every time. Repeat after me:
"through...though...enough...ought."
There's no rule regarding the letter combinations. You must look at the dictionary Pronunciation Key, which we will learn here. If you try to guess, you might be wrong three times in four tries.
If the same letters can have different sounds, so can different letters have the same sounds. Here are examples:

You eat a *pear*; you wear a *pair* of shoes; and you *pare* the skin from a potato.

All three words have the identical sound: "pair." Say "pair." (LISTEN. REPEAT ALL WORDS, IF NECESSARY.)
And of course you recognize this group of words which you already use regularly.

I am going *to* the theatre; and if you wish to go, *too*, then I will make *two* reservations.
Because small differences in sound can produce substantial differences in meaning, you can often confuse other people even when you know exactly what you mean, and are using the proper word.
Let's look at the common word "word."

<u>Notes:</u>   <u>Tasks:</u>

PRINT:
word/ward/award

POINT TO THE CORRECT WORD AS YOU SAY IT

PRINT:
context

SPECIAL SECTION: Continue On
— PAGE 11 FOR NON-NATIVE STUDENTS or
— PAGE 13 FOR AMERICAN-BORN STUDENTS

If you try to say "word" with the letter "O" sound, you are really pronouncing the English word "ward," which is a large room in a hospital. And if you attempt to say "a word' with this "O" sound, you make your listener understand "award," which is a prize.

By now you should understand that guessing is often the worst mistake you can make when learning new words. While you are in this class, I'd like you to forget your own language and its rules for vowel sounds. Your rules may not work in English pronunciation.

The process of communication by spoken language is extremely complicated. The brain must work very hard to make sense out of a stream of sounds and silences. The task is made much more difficult—and sometimes, even impossible—if you do not provide *familiar* sounds which the listener's ears *expect* in the *context* of the sentence you are speaking.

"Context" means the sense of the surrounding material. Say "context."
(LISTEN: REPEAT.)

Notes: Tasks:

INDICATE ONE PERSON FROM THE LARGEST SINGLE
LANGUAGE-GROUP IN THE CLASS. WAIT FOR THE STUDENT TO
FINISH PRINTING. TO BE FAIR, IF POSSIBLE, PICK A LANGUAGE YOU
DON'T KNOW.

**IF YOU ARE SURE OF THE DIACRITICAL MARKINGS, PLACE THEM
OVER THE FOREIGN VOWELS TO AID YOURSELF. OTHERWISE JUST
LISTEN AND IMITATE.**

**MAKE AN HONEST ATTEMPT TO PRONOUNCE THE WORD
CORRECTLY. THEN ASK:**

CONTINUE UNTIL YOU HAVE MADE FOUR TO SIX ATTEMPTS. IT IS
NOT IMPORTANT WHETHER OR NOT YOU SUCCEED, BECAUSE BOTH
CASES ARE USEFUL:
—IF YOU SUCCEED, SAY:

—IN EITHER CASE, SAY:

(SPECIAL SECTION FOR NON-NATIVE STUDENTS ONLY.)

That's why even though a *slight* accent can be charming, a *heavy* accent can make real communication slow and difficult and frustrating for everyone.

So that you understand why I will be most particular about the sounds you make in this class, I'll let you give the teacher a test.

Think of the most difficult words in your own language. I'd like somebody to print one of them on the blackboard so I can try to pronounce it.

Now pronounce that word for me. (LISTEN).
Again, please. (LISTEN).

Now let me try to say it.

Did I say it right? (PROBABLY NOT.)
Please say it again. (IMITATE.)
Is that better? Can you understand?

You see, if you really listen and apply the native speaker's own native sounds, you can duplicate the word almost exactly.

My problem is the same as your problem: small differences in sound escape the unpracticed ear. Those differences can sometimes change the meaning or make the sounds meaningless. Since you needed to correct me a few times, don't be concerned if I do that to all of you, too. Just repeat and continue. I will be coaching...not criticizing.

(END OF SPECIAL SECTION.)

(SPECIAL SECTION FOR NON-NATIVE STUDENTS ONLY.)

Notes: Tasks:

**READ ALOUD THE FOLLOWING NONSENSE PHRASE,
PRONOUNCING EACH WORD CLEARLY AND CORRECTLY.**
PRACTICE FIRST: NONSENSE PHRASES ARE MORE TRICKY THAN
THEY LOOK. BUT DO TRY TO USE THE RIGHT SENTENCE
INTONATION.

**NOW READ THE "TRANSLATION" ALOUD, PAYING SPECIAL
ATTENTION TO THE PHRASING:**

NOTE: About 20 minutes of time has
elapsed at this point.

(FOR ALL STUDENTS:)

It is difficult to explain how easily an incorrect pronunciation can interfere with communication. Let me give you an example:

"A beak block cot/coat the knight's beard/own the limbo the greet maypole/inner frond jar,/on dime furry sod."

Did you understand that? (REPEAT IT, IF YOU LIKE.)

Of course not. If doesn't make sense, even though you probably know most of those words. When the sounds are not correct for the intended or expected meanings, then the ear cannot make sense out of the combination of sounds and silences.

All of the words in that sentence were common *mis*-pronunciations of words whose vowel sounds are very similar—but different! Listen:

"A big black cat/caught the nice bird/on the limb of the great maple/in our front yard,/and I'm very sad."

Correct pronunciation makes a difference, doesn't it?

Therefore, our purpose in this class will be to teach you how to reproduce the correct sounds of each word so that you can make yourself understood...always!

Do you believe you can do that? (GET RESPONSE.)

You should believe it, because it will happen if you concentrate and practice in these classes.

Now you can understand the reasons for your basic problems. Our examples should have shown you the purposes behind our general methods. So now it is time to begin the real work.

<u>Notes:</u>   <u>Tasks:</u>

NOTE: If you are NOT using Dell's
American Heritage (college) edition,
then look up all blackboard examples given
in boxes for all following items and sessions.
To avoid confusion, you must verify and/or
change the diacritical marks to conform to
the textbook you have chosen.

PRINT:
  diacritical marks
  dī-ə-krĭt-ĭ-kəl

PRINT:
  hyphen = hī-fən

PRINT:
  write: syllable
  hyphenate: syl-la-ble
  pronounce: sĭl-ə-bəl

PRINT:
  stress

Definition page _____.

PRONUNCIATION KEYS EXPLAINED

Obviously, if the *same* combination of letters can have *different* sounds... and if *different* combinations of letters can have the *same* sound...then we must have a system for indicating the *correct* sound for the given word.

Such a system does exist for English. Every dictionary has a "Pronunciation Key" printed at the front of the book. Each publisher uses a slightly different code, but all codes function in the same way.

We will learn one code from one dictionary that seems best for our purposes.

All pronunciation keys use special code marks. These special code marks are called "diacritical marks." They are essential to correct pronunciation because they tell our eyes the sound our ears expect to hear in a conversation. Diacritical marks tell us exactly which sound to use for each portion of any given word.

Say "diacritical marks." (ALL STUDENTS MUST REPEAT.)

Say "hyphen." (AGAIN, ALL STUDENTS MUST REPEAT.)
You can see that I separated certain letter groups with hyphens. These letter groups are pronounced together. They are known as syllables.

Say, "syllable."
When a word has *more* than one syllable, English stresses *one* syllable strongly. There can be one or more *weaker* stresses, depending on the length of the word. Say "stress." (ALL REPEAT)

Next time, we will learn more about stress marks; but for today, we will spend time on the pronunciation of the symbols in the dictionary Pronunciation Key.

Notes: Tasks:

HOLD UP YOUR DICTIONARY. OPEN IT TO THE MAIN 'PRONUNCIATION KEY' SECTION AT THE FRONT OF THE BOOK. SHOW IT TO THE STUDENTS. ALSO SHOW THE VOWEL KEY AT THE FOOT OF ALL EVEN NUMBERED PAGES.

```
PRINT:
 unpredictable
```

Definition: Page _____.

```
PRINT:
 unabridged
 abridged
```

NOTE: This is the single most critical skill to be learned in the course.

GROUP EXERCISE: LEAD A RECITATION OF THE COMPLETE ALPHABET. YOU WILL HEAR MAJOR DISCREPANCIES CLEARLY, IF ANY. CORRECT THE CLASS BEFORE CONTINUING. DO NOT ACCUSE INDIVIDUALS OF ERROR—JUST CORRECT THE GROUP.

The correct pronunciation of American English is very *unpredictable*. Is that a new word for you?

Even highly educated native speakers must consult the dictionary when learning new words—so don't be embarrassed to look in the dictionary.

Unabridged (meaning "complete") English dictionaries contain more than a quarter of a million listings. Nobody knows or uses all English words. In fact, most adults know and use only about 20,000 words in their daily lives.

Therefore, most dictionaries intended for everyday reference contain only about 50,000 words. This abridged (or "shortened") paperback version is easy to carry and will contain most of the words you will need for daily life. Occasionally you won't find a word you are looking for. Then consult the unabridged book.

Although a different dictionary's diacritical marks may be slightly different, the process remains exactly the same as what we'll learn here in class: Compare the markings of new words with the markings of familiar key words.

Today, and in the next few classes, we will learn to form the specific sounds indicated by the diacritical code markings. Then you will understand the slogan of this class: "Speak English with your ears, not with your eyes!"

Before we begin, let's be sure that everyone pronounces the letters of the alphabet correctly.

That's good. The letters have names, of course, but they also have sounds. The sounds are not always the same. That is especially true of the "vowels."

Notes: Tasks:

> PRINT: "Vowels"
> A, E, I, O, U, Y

NOTE: If space permits, stretch all six letters across the top of the blackboard. If not, use oversized chart paper sheets taped to walls. (Save such sheets for review during the second session.)

TO BEGIN TEACHING THE VOWEL SOUNDS, PRINT THE FOLLOWING BLOCKS OF INFORMATION ON THE BLACKBOARD, SEGMENT BY SEGMENT, AS GIVEN BELOW. DO NOT EXPOSE THE ENTIRE ARRAY OF DIACRITICAL MARKS AT ONE TIME BECAUSE THAT IS MUCH TOO INTIMIDATING. JUST PROCEED WITH ONE LETTER-GROUP AT A TIME, UNTIL ALL HAVE BEEN COVERED.

PRONOUNCE EACH 'KEY WORD' FOR THE CLASS TO IMITATE. REPEAT SEVERAL TIMES, UNTIL THE CLASS AS A WHOLE CAN REPRODUCE AN ACCEPTABLE VOWEL SOUND. SOUNDS NEED NOT BE PERFECT TODAY SINCE THEY WILL BE TAUGHT, IF NECESSARY, IN THE SECOND SESSION.

BUDGET YOUR TIME. WITH 50+ ITEMS TO LIST (IN OVER TWENTY GROUPINGS) YOU CAN SPEND ONLY ABOUT ONE MINUTE ON EACH MARK AND ITS KEY WORD (THAT IS, 4-5 MINUTES MAXIMUM FOR THE ENTIRE DISCUSSION REGARDING THE LETTER "A.")

> PRINT:
> ‾ = bar
> ˘ = arc
> ^ = tent
> ¨ = dots

VOWEL SOUNDS

These six letters together can be marked in nineteen different ways. In addition, we have a number of "diphthongs" and "ligatures"—specific combinations of letters that represent additional sounds. In order to speak English correctly...to understand other people and to be understood by them...you must be able to reproduce about forty-five sounds accurately. That is what makes English so complicated.

These are the special code marks used with vowel sounds. Say, "bar...arc...tent...dots." (ALL REPEAT) In our dictionary, the dots are used only with the letter "A". We will learn the other indicators, now.

Notes: Tasks:

> PRINT: "A"
> ā = late
> ă = cat
> â = care
> ä = father

IN THIS AND ALL FOLLOWING SEQUENCES, REPEAT UNTIL THEIR IMITATIONS ARE ACCEPTABLY CLOSE TO CORRECT; THAT IS, NOT CONFUSED WITH OTHER SOUNDS.

WORK WITH THE SOUNDS AS A GROUP. DO NOT TAG ANY INDIVIDUAL WITH AN ERROR. THROUGHOUT THIS COURSE, IF ANYONE SEEMS TO BE HAVING PARTICULAR DIFFICULTIES, ASK THEM TO STAY AFTER CLASS FOR INDIVIDUAL HELP.

NOTE: Appendix A contains instructional information permitting you to teach the mechanics of proper sound formation for many of the most difficult sounds.

Do not "instruct" until next session, but for your own best understanding, read Appendix A while preparing for your first session.

THE METHOD OF PRESENTATION USED WITH THE LETTER "A" ABOVE IS THE MODEL FOR ALL VOWEL SOUNDS, DIPHTHONGS, AND LIGATURES THAT FOLLOW IN THIS SESSION. **ADAPT YOUR SPEED AND THE NUMBER OF REPETITIONS OF WORDS TO THE NEEDS AND ABILITIES OF YOUR GROUP.**

Any vowel with a straight bar above it has the sound of its own name. For example, in the word "late," the "A" with-the-bar is pronounced like its name. Please repeat: "late." (ALL REPEAT)

When an "A" carries a small arc, we hear the sound in the word "cat." (ALL REPEAT.)

When the "A" has a tent over it, we hear the sound in the word "care." (ALL REPEAT)

The correct sound of an American English letter "R" is difficult for many people. Do the best you can, right now. We will discuss and practice the "R" sound later.

When an "A" has two dots above it, it has the sound of the "A" in "father." (ALL REPEAT)

Just to be sure we understand. There are four main sounds for the letter "A". These are (POINT) "late," "cat," "care," "father." (ALL REPEAT.)

Don't be concerned that your sounds are not exactly right today. There will be plenty of practice for all these sounds and words in the future sessions.

For today, concentrate on the differences in the sounds I am modeling for you. Try to imitate me as closely as you can...but we will not spend too much time with any individual sound because it is more important to *hear* them *all* today.

Notes: Tasks:

PRINT: "E"
ē = see
ĕ = ten
er = ûr (stressed)
er = ər (unstressed)

ADD:
her = hûr
butter = but'ər

PRINT: "I"
ī = tie
ĭ = sit
î = pier

ADD:
bird = bûrd
ski = skē

REVIEW THE "A" AND "E" KEY WORDS IN A RANDOM PATTERN. ALWAYS GUIDE THE STUDENTS TOWARD PERFECTION BY SAYING EACH WORD FIRST, AS A MODEL FOR THEIR IMITATION.

With-a-bar above, the "E" says its own name, as in the word "see." (ALL REPEAT.)

With-an-arc, the "E" is pronounced as in the word "pen." (ALL REPEAT.)

The *American Heritage Dictionary* prints "ûr" to represent an "er" combination when it occurs in stressed syllables, as it does in the word "her." Syllables not stressed use the "schwa-R," for example, as in the word "butt**er**."

Don't be confused if the letters used for spelling and pronunciation are different. I have already told you that our words do not always sound the way they look.

When written with-a-bar, the "I" says its own name: "tie." (ALL REPEAT).

With-an-arc, we say "sit." (ALL REPEAT.)

With-a-tent, we say "pier." (ALL REPEAT.)

Now, quickly for review: "tie," "sit," "pier." (ALL REPEAT)

The American Heritage dictionary often uses "ûr" to represent a stressed "ir" combination. Say "first...stir...bird." (ALL REPEAT.)

Also, it can show an "I" pronounced as an "E." Say "ski...medium." (ALL REPEAT.)

Notes: Tasks:

PRINT: "O"
ō = go
ŏ = hot
ô = fought, for

PRINT: "U"
ū = use = yo͞o
ŭ = mud
û = urge

ADD:
û r = term, word,
           sir, heard

PRINT: "Y"
y = yes
y = ī in sky
y = ē in fairly

**REVIEW ALL THREE SOUNDS FOR THE "Y". THEN
REVIEW ALL PREVIOUS SOUNDS, AT RANDOM.** THE CLASS
SHOULD BE BECOMING FAIRLY ACCURATE AT IMITATING YOU. THE
EXERCISES IN THE NEXT SESSION WILL PROVIDE OPPORTUNITY FOR
REVIEW AND REINFORCEMENT.

With-a-bar, the "O" sounds as it does in the word "go." (ALL REPEAT.)
With-an-arc, it is the sound in "hot."(ALL REPEAT.)
And with-a-tent, it is the sound in "fought" and "for." (REPEAT AND REVIEW.)
Note that vowels in front of the letter "R" often sound slightly different. Say, "fought" and "for."

Some dictionaries use the "U" with-a-bar to show the name sound as in the word "use" or "you." The American Heritage dictionary uses "yoo" with-a-bar over it, for the name sound. You should learn both of these symbols.
The "U" with-an-arc, is pronounced as in the word "mud." (ALL REPEAT.)
The "U" with-a-tent, is the same as in the word "urge." (REPEAT AND REVIEW.)

Note that the "U" with-a-tent is used for the pronunciation of many vowels in front of the "R" sound in stressed syllables. Say, (AND POINT TO THE WORDS ON THE BOARD) "term," "word," "sir," "heard." (ALL REPEAT.)

When the dictionary shows a letter "Y" it is always pronounced like the initial sound in words such as "yes," "yet," and "yesterday." (ALL REPEAT.)
However, the letter "Y" can also have the vowel sound of an "I" as in "sky" or of the "E" as in the word "fairly." When it has the "I" or "E" sound, the dictionary prints the "I" or "E" with-the-bars above them. Say, "sky," "fairly."

To summarize: It is easier to remember the sounds with the diacritical marks if you remember that the *bar always* sounds like the vowel letter name.

<u>Notes:</u>   <u>Tasks:</u>

WHEN SATISFIED WITH THEIR PROGRESS, CONTINUE.

```
PRINT:
"schwa"  =  "ə"
(appears as an upside-down "e")
```

PRONOUNCE
as in "the" or "but"

NOTE: You may want to review the
information on the use and production of the
schwa sound which appears in Appendix A.

```
PRINT:
"ə+r"  =  mother, doctor,
                 murmur, dollar
```

```
PRINT:   ə=
onion, edible,
apply, item, circus.
```

```
PRINT: the
         thə book
         thē apple
```

```
PRINT:
 bottle  =  bot 'l
 bottom  =bot 'əm
 button  =but 'n
 duchess  =  duch 'ĭs
```

———   ———

THE SCHWA VOWEL

In addition to the many vowel sounds of the six letters we have just reviewed, American English has one more sound that we call the "schwa." It is a neutral, breathy sound that we often use as a filler between consonants in unstressed syllables. This is particularly true when a vowel is followed by an "R" and occurs at the end of a word such as "mother," "doctor," "murmur," "dollar."

The schwa is also used for different vowels in unstressed syllables of words when the "R" sound is *not* present. Say "onion, edible, apply, item, circus."

The schwa sound is also used in the common article "the" when used before a consonant. Say "the book," "the knife," "the shoes." (ALL REPEAT.) That's good.

However, when used before a word beginning with a vowel, the article "the" is pronounced "thee" (thē). Say "the apple," "the office," "the orange ball." (REPEAT.)

In some dictionaries, the schwa sound appears as an apostrophe or a very small symbol between consonants, especially at the ends of words. In the American Heritage Dictionary, the stress mark sometimes replaces the apostrophe. The effect is the same—we slide past the vowel. For example:

Notes: Tasks:

> **PRINT:**
> Speak English with your ears,
> not with your eyes.

NOTE: Take a one-minute stretch break.
(About 40-50 minutes total time have elapsed to
this point.)

NOTE: Jot down any particular problems
noticed during this exercise so you can give
special attention in the Second Session.

_____

_____

_____

_____

_____

_____

_____

_____

When you see an "L," "M," "S," or "N" standing alone, after a stressed syllable, remember to say the sound and not the letter name. These sounds often end words with or without the schwa sound. Say "bottle, bottom, button, duchess." (ALL REPEAT.)

To summarize: This completes the group of simple vowel sounds. You have just learned about twenty different sounds for the six vowel letters in English; and all those sounds are very accurately represented by the diacritical codes.

Twenty possible sounds from six letters—that is part of the reason you might be having a problem with English pronunciation and conversation.

And that is why we say, "Speak English with your ears, not with your eyes."

Notes: Tasks:

> PRINT: "R"

> PRINT: "R" = are

NOTE: The technical name for the American "R" is the retroflex-R.

NOTE: Be patient. Most students will not be able to reproduce the "R" sound perfectly on the first day of class...if ever.

NOTE: An optional review section for the American-R appears in Appendix A after the discussion of its sound production.

NOTE: If for any reason you must break the First Session into two parts, this is the best break point. For reasons discussed in the Preface, we recommend one long class covering all the sounds of the language.

DEALING WITH THE LETTER "R"

The correct pronunciation of the "R" sound is the same as its name and as in the word "are." Say "R". . ."are." (ALL REPEAT.)

The American-R sound is made back in your throat and with the tip of the tongue. The back of your tongue should squeeze your throat as if you were about the make a "K" or "G" sound. Say, "cake, go." (ALL REPEAT.) Notice where the back of your tongue is.

Let's practice in easy steps:

First say "aaahhh" (ALL REPEAT.)

Now, while you are still making the "aaahhh" sound, squeeze your throat with the back of your tongue, then make the tip of your tongue curl at the gum ridge—BUT DO NOT LET IT TOUCH THE GUM RIDGE.

That is how we form our word "are." You are beginning to say the letter "R" correctly.

<u>Notes:</u>   <u>Tasks:</u>

PRINT:
 diphthong
 dĭf-thŏng

PRINT:
 oi/oy
 oil
 example: boy = boi

ADD:
 au/ou/ow
 cow/out
 our/hour
 example: cow = kou

PRINT:
 bow—noun
 bō=gō
 bow—verb
 bow=bou
 how=hou

DIPHTHONGS AND LIGATURES

In addition to the six basic vowel letters and the schwa sound, standard American English uses other complex sounds created by the combination of two or more vowels. This combination of sounds, gliding from one into another, is called a diphthong.

The Greek root of this word means "two voices." We hear two vowel sounds in the three diphthong combinations which occur in most dialects of English: **oi**, **au**, and **ai**.

Say, "oil" (ALL REPEAT.)...Say "boy." (ALL REPEAT.) Our dictionary represents this sound with "**oi**."

The glide from one sound into another is also very clear with words spelled with "OU" and "OW. " Say "out" (ALL REPEAT.) Say "cow." (ALL REPEAT.) Our dictionary represents this sound with "OU." Say "how...towel." (ALL REPEAT.)

The word b-o-w can sound like the bow in your shoe laces or a bow to your dancing partner, depending on whether you are using the noun or verb form and how you pronounce it. Therefore the dictionary does not print the "W" unless it has a "W" sound at the beginning of a word.

Check your dictionary—every time.

Notes: Tasks:

NOTE: Linguists also consider the "ai"
combination to be a diphthong, but our
dictionary represents this sound with the
letter "I", its name sound.

```
PRINT:
ai = ī
```

```
ADD:
 Thailand
 kaiser
```

```
PRINT: "oo" diphthong
 o͝o = foot
 o͞o = food
```

```
PRINT: "oo" spelling
 door = dôr
 flood = flŭd
```

In the dictionary, the diphthong "ai" is always printed with the single letter "I" with-a-bar. Say "Thailand...kaiser." (ALL REPEAT.)

In addition to the diphthong, in which you hear two sounds, English dictionaries also use a vowel ligature, in which two vowels are joined to form a new sound. The double-O is such a ligature.

What is complicated is that the double-O ligature can have any of four standard sounds. Here they are:

When the double-O carries the arc, the new sound is like the sound in "foot." (ALL REPEAT.) That sound also occurs in "book...took...look...soot." (ALL REPEAT.)

It is also the "OU" sound in such words as "could, would, and should." Say, "would...could...should." (ALL REPEAT.)

When the double-O carries the bar, then the sound changes to the sound in "food." Do you hear the difference?

Listen: "Foot/food...could/cool." (ALL REPEAT.)

Other words with the double-O and the bar are:
"tool...fool...school...soothe." (ALL REPEAT ALL WORDS UNTIL SOUNDS ARE FAIRLY ACCURATE.)

Some words in English are *spelled* with a double-O but are *not pronounced* like "foot," or "food.

Look at the word "door." It is spelled with a double-O but is pronounced the same as "for," and in the dictionary is printed with the "O" with-a-tent.

"Flood" also is spelled with a double-O but is pronounced like the word "mud," and the dictionary uses a "U" with-an-arc over it for the double-O.

To be sure we recognize all four sounds, let's review:
"foot...food...door...flood." (ALL REPEAT.)

Notes: Tasks:

ADD: "ū" = "yo͞o"
 you = yo͞o
 cute = kyo͞ot or kūt
 beauty = byo͞o-tē or bū-tē
 fuel =fyo͞o-əl or fū-əl

Always use your dictionary when you see a double-O because, as you can hear, you have one chance to be correct, and three chances to be wrong!

Do you have any questions? (ANSWER FULLY.)

The arc and the bar are the only two diacritical marks used with the double-O diphthong, because the sound for the letter "U" is accompanied by the letter "Y plus double-O." Say, "you...cute...beauty...fuel." (ALL REPEAT.)

Notes: Tasks:

PRINT: consonant
kŏn-sə-nənt

NOTE: The technical name for throat sounds is "glottal" sounds.

PRINT:
ligature
lĭg-ə-chər

CONSONANTS AND CONSONANT LIGATURES

Consonants are generally considered to be all the sounds of the language except the vowels. Sometimes they are further categorized according to whether the sound is formed predominantly with the lips, the tongue and the teeth, or the throat.

A ligature is a two-letter combination used by dictionaries to indicate one standardized sound. The word *ligature* means to bind or tie. Applied to the language, it means a combination of letters that symbolize a new sound *only when that combination is used together.* The double-O, just discussed, is a vowel ligature.

Most other ligatures are formed with either two consonants or one consonant combined with one vowel.

Because these ligature symbols and sounds are so important to the correct pronunciation of English, we will practice them as often as we practice vowels, in future classes.

Because some ligatures are voiced, we will begin with a general discussion of voiced consonants.

Notes: Tasks:

PRINT:
s/z

ADD:
f/v, t/d, p/b, k/g

ADD:
j/ch, sh/zh

ADD:
th/**th**

VOICING

Pairs of similar consonants in English are distinguished by the use of voicing for one of the two consonants in each pair.

These special pairs include the "S" and "Z"...

the "F" and "V," the "T" and "D," the "P" and "B," the "K" and "G"...

the "J" and the ligatures "ch," "sh" and "zh"...

and the two "th" ligatures.

We have separated these pairs because each of the four groups shares certain characteristics *besides* voicing.

Notes: Tasks:

```
┌─────────────────────────┐
│ PRINT: (or circle):     │
│ s/z                     │
└─────────────────────────┘
```

NOTE: Point to your mouth when you make an "S" sound and to your throat when you make the "Z" sound.

VOICED SIBILANT PAIR

Voicing is the only difference between the hissing sound of the letter "S" and the buzzing sound of the letter "Z." Listen: s-s-s-s-s, z-z-z-z-z-, s-s-s-s-s, z-z-z-z-z.

Let me hear you make these sounds: s-s-s-s-s...z-z-z-z-z...s-s-s-s-s... z-z-z-z-z. (ALL REPEAT.)

Now put your fingers on your throat and repeat those same sounds. Say, s-s-s-s-s...z-z-z-z-z. (ALL REPEAT.) Say, "so/zone...sip/zip." (ALL REPEAT.)

The vibrations you feel in your fingers when you make the "Z" sound are the result of voicing. This addition of voicing is what makes the difference in half of each of the other pairs also.

We will return to the other "sibilant" sounds in a few minutes.

Notes: Tasks:

```
┌─────────────────────────────┐
│ PRINT (or circle):          │
│ f/v                         │
└─────────────────────────────┘
```

NOTE: Point to the mouth and the throat as appropriate.

```
┌─────────────────────────────┐
│ ADD:                        │
│   ferry/very                │
│   fast/vast                 │
└─────────────────────────────┘
```

VOICED LABIO-DENTAL PAIRS

Exactly the same difference exists between the "F" sound and the "V" sound. Put your fingers on your throat and make these sounds: f-f-f-f-f... v-v-v-v-v.(ALL REPEAT.)

Say, "ferry, very." (ALL REPEAT.) Say, "fast...vast." (ALL REPEAT.)
These two pairs (the s/z and the f/v), are easy to make because we can create a fairly continuous sound. Because that is not possible with the next group we must be aware of what our throat is doing.

Notes: Tasks:

PRINT (or circle):
t/d, p/b, k/g

NOTE: Speech professionals use the term "plosives," but most students already understand "explosive" and will grasp the concept more quickly.

NOTE: When modeling these sounds for the students to imitate, take care to use the sound (with schwa), not the letter name. In the first demonstration, you might over-emphasize the force of air; but the class should work with normal plosive force, stressing the voicing for the appropriate half of each pair.

PRINT:
time/dime
pin/bin
kilt/guilt

PRINT:
bed/bet
hog/hawk

VOICED EXPLOSIVE PAIRS

Three pairs of consonants are called "explosive" sounds. These sounds have one common characteristic: that is, the basic sound is formed in the same way for both halves of each pair: both begin with a puff of air, especially when they begin the word.

The difference, again, is voicing. As I mentioned, we cannot hold a continuous sound with very many consonants. So, put your fingers to your throat again. If you are making the second sound correctly in each pair, you should be able to feel your throat vibrate with the "D," "B," and "G."

Using the schwa sound, let's hear these pairs: "t/d, p/b, k/g."

Say, "time...dime." (ALL REPEAT.)
Say, "pin...bin." (ALL REPEAT.)
Say, "kilt...guilt." (ALL REPEAT.)
Usually the distinction is clear when any of these letter pairs begins a word, because we put energy into the beginning of words.

However, problems can occur when these same sounds end a word, because many people "swallow" the last syllable of many words.

Think of the great difference in meanings between "making a bed" and "making a bet"...or between "hog" and "hawk."

Notes: Tasks:

```
PRINT:
 t/d = plant/planned
 p/b = cap/cab
 k/g = tack/tag
```

NOTE: It is true that in our normal speech
patterns many native speakers do not
generally emphasize word endings.
Nevertheless, we do take care to emphasize,
to enunciate, key sounds in words that are
easily misunderstood.

Now let's use these same pairs with words that *end,* rather than *begin,* with these sounds.

Say, "plant/planned...cap/cab...tack/tag." (ALL REPEAT.)

We need to speak quite distinctly if we want people to understand. Because misunderstandings can occur so easily, it is easier and wiser to pronounce all words clearly the first time.

Notes:

NOTE: These sounds are technically called sibilants and include the S, Z, sh, zh, ch, and J sounds.

NOTE: See Appendix A for the production of sibilant sounds.

> PRINT:
> sh/zh

> PRINT:
> shoe, shirt
> cash, dish

NOTE: As before, point to the mouth and throat as you model "S" and "Z" variations to get the "sh" and the "zh" sounds. Check Appendix A for a description of the "S" and "sh" production.

> PRINT:
> ge = zh
> beige = bāzh
> garage = gə-räzh′

> PRINT:
> su = zh
> leisure = lē′zhər
> pleasure = plĕ′zhər
> casual = kăzh′ o͞o-əl

THE FAMILY OF "S" SOUNDS

Now let us return to the "S" and "Z" sounds.

You will recall that no one had difficulty in adding voicing to the "S" sound to create the "Z" sound. That was probably true because both sounds occur in most other languages, as well.

Exactly the same voicing principle is at work with the "sh" and "zh" ligatures, too.

The "sh" ligature sound is easy. Say, sh-sh-sh-sh-sh." (ALL REPEAT.) Again, make and hold the same sound: sh-sh-sh-sh-sh. (ALL REPEAT.)

Say, "shoe...shirt...cash...dish." (ALL REPEAT.)

Now add the same voicing that you would add to the letter "Z." Feel the vibration in your throat? Say, "zh-zh-zh-zh-zh." (ALL REPEAT.) Say "sh-sh-sh-sh-sh, zh-zh-zh-zh-zh, sh-sh-sh-sh-sh." (ALL REPEAT.) Do you hear the difference?

The "zh" ligature is a *created* symbol. That is, we do not find that spelling in English words. It might occur in a foreign word printed in a book or newspaper, but that is an exception.

Two main letter combinations usually represent the "zh" sound.

One combination is the word-ending "ge." It can have several sounds, including the "zh." Say, "beige...garage." (ALL REPEAT.)

The "zh" sound is also formed by the "su" combination in some words.

Say, "leisure...pleasure...casual." (ALL REPEAT.)

The "su" combination can be tricky because it has two other sounds as well. One is the simple sound of the consonant "S" and the vowel, used together.

Notes: Tasks:

PRINT:
 su = "su"
 super = o͞o
 supper = ŭ
 suffer = ŭ
 suit = o͞o

PRINT:
 su = "sh"
 sugar
 sure

PRINT: "sh" ligature
 sh = shoe, cash
 su = sure, sugar
 si = mission, passion
 ch = machine, Chicago
 ci = appreciate, special
 ti = nation, ratio

PRINT:
 -tion = shən

PRINT:
 sh/zh
 ch/j

NOTE: See Appendix A for the production of these sounds.

Say, "super...supper...suffer...suit." (ALL REPEAT.)
The third common pronunciation of "su" is that of the "sh" ligature.

Say, "sure...sugar." (ALL REPEAT.)
The dictionary also prints the "sh" ligature as the correct pronunciation for several other two-letter combinations in commonly used words:

Repeat after me: "shoe/cash...sure/sugar...mission/passion...machine/Chicago...appreciate/special...nation/ration." (ALL REPEAT.)
Of course, all of these combinations can also be heard as the regular consonant-vowel combination. To be sure, you must check the dictionary.
The "ti" combination is extremely important because it is found in many nouns ending in "tion," pronounced "shən."

Very closely related to the "sh" ligature sound are two other sounds. One is the result of an explosive force of air added to the "sh" ligature, and the other is the result of adding voicing to the explosive form. This group might surprise you.

Notes: Tasks:

PRINT: "ch" ligature
cheese = chēz
children = chil 'drən
lunch = lŭnch

PRINT: "J"
joke
major
jewel
just
jump

PRINT: "J"
dg = edge = ĕj
         pledge = plĕj
         judge = jŭj

ADD: "J"
du = educate
       ĕj 'ə-kāt

       adulation
       ăj 'ōō lā 'shən

ADD:
adult = ə-dŭlt '
duty = dōō 'te

ADD: "G" = "J"
gem = jĕm
merge = mûrj
gin = jĭn
gym = jĭm

These are all words you probably use frequently. Say, "cheese...children...lunch." (ALL REPEAT.)

The "J" sound is simply the "ch" sound with voicing added. Feel the vibration in your throat as you say the following words.

Say, "joke...major...jewel...just...jump." (ALL REPEAT.)

As you have already guessed, there are other letter combinations with which we spell the "J" sound.

Sometimes the "dg" combination is pronounced like the "J" sound. Say, "edge...pledge...judge." (ALL REPEAT.)

Sometimes a "du" combination is pronounced like a "J" sound. Say, "educate...adulation." (ALL REPEAT.)

Be careful of the more common use of "du," which is pronounced with a "D" as in the words "duty" and "adult." Say, "adult...duty." (ALL REPEAT.)

The "J" sound is also heard with many words that contain the letter "G" in combination with the vowel sounds "E," "I," or "Y."

As you have seen, the letter "G" can also be pronounced as it is in the words "go" and "dog," or as a "zh" sound in the words "beige" and "garage," or as the "J" in "gin" and "gem." Don't guess. Always check your dictionary. The proper sound will be represented by a "G" or a "zh" or a "J" symbol, appropriate for the given word.

Notes:

Tasks:

```
PRINT: "th"
  think
  thank you
```

NOTE: These two common words, "think" and "thank you," are made by letting the air escape between the flat top of the tongue and your upper teeth. Both are voiceless.

```
ADD:
  bath
  teeth
  cloth
  thick
  thin
```

```
PRINT: "th"
  these
  those
  that
  mother/father
  bathing
  clothing
```

NOTE: Show the voiced "th" ligature on the blackboard by underlining all those ligatures printed above and following shown in boldface type.

NOTE: Repeat the voiceless sounds also, until all are acceptably close to correct. As easy as these sounds are to make, many students will have difficulty hearing or making the difference between the voiced and voiceless sounds. Have them hold the sounds in front of words until they can hear the difference between the "th" in "think" and the "th" in "they," for example.

THE "TH" PAIR

Voicing is also the key to the two sounds of the "th" ligature.

Let me hear you do it. Say, "th-th-th-th-th." (ALL REPEAT.) Now say "think...thank you." (ALL REPEAT.) Notice where your tongue is.

Say, "bath...teeth...cloth...thick...thin." (ALL REPEAT.)

When we add voicing to the "th" sound, we get a throaty sound as in the words "these" and "those." Let me hear you say it: "th-th-th-th-th."

Say, "These...those...that...mother...father...bathing...clothing" (ALL REPEAT.)

Notes: Tasks:

NOTE: Make sure they feel their throat when
they make these sounds so that they can feel
the difference as well as hear it.

> PRINT:
>   underlining = voicing

> ADD:
>   bold face (thick) = voicing
>   *italics* = voicing

NOTE: About 90 minutes total time have
elapsed to this point.

Here are some pairs of words that use both sounds. Say, "bath/bathing...
cloth/clothing...north/northern." Can you hear and feel the difference? Say,
"bath...bathing...cloth...clothing...north...northern."
(ALL REPEAT.)

Notice that I have used underlining to indicate voicing. Some dictionaries
also use underlining or boldface (thicker) type. Our dictionary uses italics for the
voiced "th" sound. Italics are thin, slanted letters. Because it is difficult to show
italics with chalk, I will continue to underline the "th" ligature when voicing is
needed.

Notes: Tasks:

NOTE: The "ng" ligature is called the "eng" sound.

```
PRINT:
  "eng" sound = ng
  "eng" sound = ŋ
```

NOTE: Some dictionaries use the symbol "ŋ" for the "eng" sound.

```
PRINT: "ng" ligature
  -ing/sing
  -ang/sang
  -ong/song
  -ung/sung
  -eng/length
```

```
PRINT: "ing" = ng
  verb + -ing
  going
  talking
  playing
```

```
PRINT:
  ng ligature
  means "No G."
```

```
ADD: eng-eng
  sing/singing
  bring/bringing
```

NOTE: Continue, making sure the "G" sound is gone from all students.

THE "NG" LIGATURE

Whenever our dictionary shows the "ng" ligature, you know the sound is the "eng" without the "G" sound. The "eng" sound can be combined with all the vowel sounds.

Say, "sing...sang...song...sung...length." (ALL REPEAT.)
Also, remember that all verbs have an "ing" form which contains the "eng" sound printed with the "ng" ligature.

Say, "go/going...talk/talking...play/playing." (ALL REPEAT.)
An easy way to remember the correct sound of the printed "ng" ligature is this: "ng" ligature means "No G."

It is also possible to have a double-eng sound.

Say, "sing/singing...bring/bringing." (ALL REPEAT.)
Remember not to pronounce the "G" in the middle of the word or at the end. Say "eng": "sing/singing...bring/bringing." (ALL REPEAT.)

Notes: Tasks:

PRINT:
n + k = ng + k
ink = ĭngk
thank you = thăngk yōō

PRINT:
n + g = ng + g
anger = ăng-gər
hunger = hŭng-gər

ADD: (for review)
n + g = (no "G")
singer/hanger

PRINT:
uncle = ŭng′kəl

NOTE: Make sure you get an "eng" sound plus the "K." There is an optional lesson for the "ng + K" in Appendix A.

Now that you have learned *not* to make the "G" sound with the "ng" ligature, we will learn some exceptions.

When the dictionary shows the "ng" symbol followed by the letters "G" or "K," *both* the "eng" *and* the letters "G" or "K" are pronounced.

Say, "ink...thank you." (ALL REPEAT.)

Sometimes, words with the "N" followed by a "G" include the "G" sound. Part of the problem for non-native speakers is that these words are very common in daily use. But, because they are learned by imitation in unpredictable circumstances, the sounds are not always learned as a tutor would teach them. Once learned incorrectly, pronunication is difficult to change. So you will need to practice. Here are some examples:

Say, "anger." Remember to say the "eng" *and* the "G" sound with this word. (ALL REPEAT.) Say, "angry...hunger...finger...linger." (ALL REPEAT.)

The "er" ending does not determine sounds.

Say, "singer...hanger." (ALL REPEAT. MAKE SURE THE "G" IS MISSING.)

The lesson: you must check the pronunciation code printed in the dictionary.

The rule, if there is one, is that you do not hear the "G" or "K" sounds with the "ing" or "er" ending unless they are also heard in the basic word. This is important to remember because most abridged (shortened) dictionaries, including ours, do not give separate entries to word endings.

One last note about exceptions with the "eng" sound.

In a few words, such as "uncle," the letter "C" sounds like a "K" and will function like the "eng + K" rule. The dictionary will print "ngk." Say "uncle." (ALL REPEAT.)

Notes: Tasks:

> **PRINT:**
> stranger = strān′jər
> plunger = plŭn′jər

NOTE: Jot down any particular problems
noticed during this exercise so you can give
special attention in the Second Session.

_____

_____

_____

_____

_____

_____

_____

_____

_____

_____

Finally, there are also words that are spelled with an "ng" combination but are not pronounced with an "eng" sound.

Say, "stranger...plunger." (ALL REPEAT.) These words use the "J" sound instead of the "eng" sound. Again say, "stranger...plunger." (ALL REPEAT.)

Notice that with both exceptions ("uncle" and "stranger"), the dictionary code tells you exactly how to pronounce these words.

No matter how unusual the difference seems between spelling and pronunciation, trust the dictionary. It is never wrong!

Notes: Tasks:

PRINT: "G" sounds
gum/gem/beige

PRINT: "C"
c = s: certain, place
c = k: cup/act
c = s or k: circus, circle
c = ch: cello

NOTE: The word "cello" is borrowed from Italian, and we pronounce the "C" as a "ch", the same as if we were speaking Italian.

ADD
cellophane
sel′ə -fān

PRINT:
cc = ks: success
cc = k: accord

PRINT:
x = ks: extra
x = gz: exit
x = z: xylophone

TRICKY LETTERS AND SOUNDS

As we have just seen, a few letters or combinations of letters have a variety of sounds not necessarily related to simple rules. We have already shown the variety of sounds the letter "G" can be pronounced as. Say, "gum/gem/beige." (ALL REPEAT.) Remember, the dictionary will print a "G", a "J" or a "zh" ligature, as necessary.

When the dictionary prints the letter "G," it is *always* the sound of "go" and "gum."
Consider also the letter "C."

The letter "C" is never sure whether it is an "S" or a "K." But the dictionary tells you by printing an "S" or a "K." Say, "certain...place...cup... act...circus...circle." (ALL REPEAT.)

Say, "cello." (ALL REPEAT.)
However, other words spelled with the same letters are pronounced with an "S." Say, "cellophane." (ALL REPEAT.)

Many words are written with a double-C. As you might expect, there are two ways to pronounce this combination also.

Let me hear you say, "success...accord." (ALL REPEAT.)

Now let's look at the letter "X."

The letter "X" usually functions as a "ks" sound, especially when it occurs inside a word or at the end of a word. Note that the "ks" is similar to the name sound of this letter. However, in English, when an "X" begins a word it is usually pronounced like a "Z." Say, "extra...taxi...tax...xylophone." (ALL REPEAT.)

Notes: Tasks:

```
ADD:
 exit = ĕgs ′it
      = ĕks ′it
```

```
PRINT:
 qu = kw or k (beginning)
 qu = k (ending)

 quick, quiet, quota, queen
  k = quiche, quay
```

```
ADD:
 discotheque: dĭs-kō-tĕk ′
 communiqué: kə-myōō-nĭ-kā
```

```
PRINT:
 ph = f
 gh = f
 photograph = fō ′tə-grăf
 rough = rŭf
```

Sometimes the "X" is pronounced like a "G" followed by a "Z" as in the words "eggs." Say, "exit...exam...examination." You may pronounce the word "exit" with a "ks" also. Say, "eggs-it", "eks-it." The dictionary prints both alternatives.

Two last ligatures should be considered: the "qu" and the "F" sound combinations.

The "qu" combination can have either of two distinctive sounds, depending on whether it begins or ends a word.

Say, "quick...quiet...quota...queen." (ALL REPEAT.) But notice the "K" sound in "quiche" and "quay." (ALL REPEAT.)

The English language has borrowed many words from the French language, and we often pronounce the "que" in the same way the French do. Say, "discotheque...communiqué." (ALL REPEAT.)

The "F" sound is printed in the dictionary for all syllables spelled with the "ph" ligature. Usually (but not always) the dictionary prints an "F" for words spelled with "gh." For example:

Ligatures are curious because they can occur either in the spelling of a word or in the dictionary pronunciation code, but the effect is always the same: one sound from two letters, or two sounds from one letter.

Notes: Tasks:

PRINT:
often = o′fən
know = nō
hour = our
walk = wôk
bomb = bäm
time = tīm
who = ho͞o
answer = an′sər

DISAPPEARING LETTERS

Sometimes letters that are used in spelling a word are not used in pronouncing that same word.

Say, "often...know...hour...walk...bomb...time...who...answer." (ALL REPEAT.)

Notice that the dictionary simply *ignores* the unpronounced letters. You should do the same. There are many unpronounced letters in English. They occur everywhere. Sometimes native speakers mispronounce these words. Always look up new and unusual words in the dictionary and avoid saying the disappearing letters.

Notes: Tasks:

PRINT:
Thomas = tŏm'əs

PRINT:
have, help, hint,
hope, hum

PRINT: wh = h
who, whom,
hōō, hōōm

PRINT: wh = hw
which, where, white,
hwĭch, hwār, hwīt

ADD:
wear/where
witch/which

NOTE: In rapid speech, the initial "H"
sound is often dropped by even native
speakers, but the students must understand
the dictionary entry.

DEALING WITH "H" AND "WH" COMBINATIONS

The letter "H" behaves strangely and it never says its own name in a word. Sometimes it disappears.

Say, "Thomas." (ALL REPEAT.)

When correctly formed, the "H" sound is only an escape of air, with some force. We hear it most clearly when it begins a word.

Say, "have...help...hint...hope...hum." (ALL REPEAT.)

In combination with the "W," however, the letter "H" functions differently. Here it replaces the "W."

In these words the "W" disappears and the "H" becomes the key sound. Say, "who...whom." (ALL REPEAT.)

But in these words, which are spelled with "wh," the "H" sound *precedes* the "W"—that is, it appears first.

Say, "which...where...white." (ALL REPEAT.)

If the "H" sound *occurs* first, the dictionary *prints* the letter "H" first. Believe the dictionary.

Listen to the difference the "H" sound can make: Say, "wear/where... witch/which." (ALL REPEAT.)

SUMMARY

We're finished for today. That is the last of the dictionary diacritical marks and combinations of letters that could be shown with those diacritical code markings.

Next session, we will review these sounds and diacritical marks to be sure you are making the correct sound with each mark. Bring your notes to the next class period, because they will be useful.

After a few practice sessions here in class, you will begin to make sounds that are far more accurate than today...even perfect.

As your sounds improve, we will begin to work with words having multiple syllables. By the time you reach the last few sessions, you will be combining words into phrases that express meanings.

Once you recognize the value of phrasing-for-sense in communication, you will be equipped to speak English fluently. After that, you will need only practice with native-born speakers.

Do NOT practice these sounds from your notes until our next class. Because the sounds are very subtle in some cases, you could mix them up. That would create unnecessary problems. Practice only here in class.

After several more classes, the correct sounds of the dictionary will become a good habit, and you won't have to think about them. So for now, just remember our slogan: "Speak English with your ears, not with your eyes."

Notes: Tasks:

ELICIT A WORD AND PRINT IT ON THE BOARD

PRINT OTHER WORD(S).

CONTINUE AS NEEDED.

TO CONCLUDE:

FUTURE ASSIGNMENT:

PURPOSE: THE PURPOSE OF THIS SESSION IS TO FAMILIARIZE THE STUDENTS WITH THE PHONETIC KEY TO PRONUNCIATION, WITHOUT INDIVIDUAL TESTING. IF YOU DO NOT UNDERSTAND THAT CLEARLY, GO BACK AND RE-READ THE ENTIRE PRESENTATION.

IN THE SECOND SESSION, YOU WILL REVIEW AND BEGIN TO CORRECT ERRORS BY TEACHING THE MECHANICS OF PRODUCING THE CORRECT SOUNDS. HOW-TO INSTRUCTIONAL MATERIAL IS GIVEN IN APPENDIX A.

NOT UNTIL THE THIRD SESSION WILL WE TEST INDIVIDUAL RESPONSE TO THE OVERALL PRONUNCIATION CODES. THIS METHOD OF DELAYED CRITICISM WILL BEGIN TO BUILD THEIR CAPABILITY AND CONFIDENCE. DO NOT DISCOURAGE THEM BY ATTEMPTING A TOO-EARLY TEST, OR BY INSISTING ON PERFECTION TODAY. THEY WILL IMPROVE TREMENDOUSLY IN THE NEXT FEW SESSION.

GUARANTEED!!!

IF TIME REMAINS IN THE CLASS PERIOD

In the few minutes remaining, let's see whether we can help you with problem words. Do you have any word that causes you a problem? Don't pronounce it—just spell it (or write it on the board).

We say "_____." (ALL REPEAT.)

We say "_____." (ALL REPEAT.)

That is all the time we have. For next time, bring a short list of words which give you problems in pronunciation. Next time we will see exactly how the dictionary uses the diacritical marks to indicate proper pronunciation. So, we will meet in class again next _____ -day at _____am/pm. See you then. Goodbye/good night.

END OF FIRST SESSION

SECOND SESSION

SECOND SESSION

Notes: Tasks:

DURING YOUR PRELIMINARY, PRE-CLASS STUDY OF THIS TUTORING
SESSION, LIST THE MATERIALS NEEDED FOR THE CLASS HERE:

**TO SAVE CLASS TIME, GET READY TO CONDUCT A
REVIEW DRILL** BY PUTTING THE ENTIRE KEY-WORD SET (TUTOR'S
BASIC DRILL CHART, PAGE 80-81) ON THE BLACKBOARD. IF YOU ARE
USING OVERSIZED CHART PAPER, TAPE ALL ON THE WALL IN
ADVANCE OF CLASS.

DO NOT HAND OUT THE TUTOR'S BASIC DRILL CHART!
HAVING A CHART IN HAND GIVES SOME STUDENTS A FALSE SENSE
OF COMMAND, AND THEY DO NOT TRY AS HARD AS THEY
OTHERWISE MIGHT. WHEN READY TO BEGIN THE CLASS:

CONDUCT THE DRILL AS A GROUP EXERCISE. DRILL ON
THE KEY WORD SET, REPEATING EACH KEY WORD TWO OR MORE
TIMES, AS NECESSARY. LISTEN CAREFULLY AS THEY SHARPEN
THEIR EARS BY ATTEMPTING TO IMITATE YOU. EXPECT AT LEAST A
FEW "NEAR MISSES." THESE WILL IMPROVE.

ALSO EXPECT MAJOR ERRORS, BUT CORRECT THEM IMMEDIATELY,
USING PERTINENT MATERIAL FROM APPENDIX A. READ IN THE
CHART ORDER TO BUILD THEIR FAMILIARITY. ALLOW ABOUT TEN
MINUTES. WHEN MOST OF THE STUDENTS MAKE MOST OF THE
SOUNDS CORRECTLY, YOU CAN CONTINUE.

SECOND SESSION

◄——— *DURING ADVANCE PREPARATION, DO THIS*

TUTOR: You'll be glad to know that there are no more charts to copy. We finished that last time.

Today, we will review all the sounds and the diacritical marks learned last time. The full chart is on the blackboard (or chart sheets). As we review this material, compare the chart to your own notes. Correct your notes, if necessary.

Let's begin with a group review. I will model the key word, and you should repeat after me. We will pronounce every word twice if your sound is correct. If your sounds are not correct, we will repeat the problem word until it is right.

Are you ready?

PRACTICAL WORD POWER

TUTOR'S BASIC DRILL CHART*

Symbols:	A	E	I	O	U
ˉ = bar	ā = late	ē = see	ī = tie	ō = go	ū = use
˘ = arc	ă = cat	ĕ = ten	ĭ = sit	ŏ = hot	= yo͞o
ˆ = tent	â = care	er = ûr	î = pier	ô = for,	ŭ = mud
¨ = dots	ä = father	(stressed)	ir = ûr	fought	û = urge
		er = ər	(stressed)	or = ûr	ûr = term
		(unstressed)	i = ē	(word)	sir
			(ski = skē)		word
					heard

Y

y = yes
y = ī (sky)
y = ē (fairly)
and in most "ly"
adverbial endings

Schwa:
ə and ər

thə (book)
thē (apple)
ər = doctor, baker,
murmur
Sometimes: apostrophe =
ə + l,m,n,r
(in unstressed syllables;
see Appendix A)

R

Do not drill prior to
instruction in Second and
Third Sessions. (see
Appendix A) Sound is "are"

Diphthongs: (International code with English spelling equivalents)

oi	au	ai
oi = oil	ou = out, count	ai = ī
boy	how, cow	Thailand
	tower, towel	kaiser

* **NOTE:** Be sure to correct all deficiencies in
sound production. See Appendix A.

(continued on next page)

DO NOT DISTRIBUTE THIS CHART! With chart in hand, some students feel they have a magic
solution and so do not work as hard as they otherwise might.

PRACTICAL WORD POWER

TUTOR'S BASIC DRILL CHART, continued

Voiced/Voiceless Pairs:

1. **explosives:**
   - t/d = time/dime
   - p/b = pin/bin
   - k/g = kilt/guilt

2. **sibilants:**
   - s/z = so/zone
   - sh/zh = cash/casual
   - ch/j = cherry/Jerry

3. **others:**
   - f/v = ferry/very
   - th/**th** = bath/bathing

4. **relationships:**
   - exploded- sh = ch
   - exploded- zh = j

"eng" Sounds:
   See Appendix A

   - "eng" = ng ligature
   - = ŋ symbol
   - -ng = sing, sang
     song, sung
     length
   - -ng-ng = singing
     bringing
   - -ng + k = ink, thank
   - -ng + g = finger, anger

(Memory hook: "NG" in
dictionary means "No G.")

© 1989, 1987 by Richard Cavalier

Other tricky letters and sounds:

Unsure letters:
G:
- spelling "g" = gum,
  gem, beige
- dictionary "g" = go,
  gum **only.**

C:
c =	s =	place
c =	k =	cup
c =	ch =	cello
cc =	ks =	success
cc =	k =	accord

X:
x =	ks =	extra, Mexico
		Texas
x =	gz =	exit
x =	z =	xylophone

Q:
qu =	kw =	quick, quality
qu =	k =	quiche, quay
qu+ =	k =	discotheque
		communiquè

F:
ph or gh = f (printed)
   photograph, phase, phone
   laugh, tough, enough
   Philadelphia

Disappearing letters:
   - often = of ′ən
   - know = nō
   - hour = our
   - walk = wôk
   - bomb = bäm
   - time = tīm
   - who = ho͞o
   - answer = an′sər

Note: there are many other
words students will know;
some are reviewed in the
Third Session.

Letter "H" behaviors:

—disappears	=	Thomas
		ghost
—begins	=	have
		help
—replaces	=	who
	=	ho͞o
—precedes	=	which
	=	hwĭch*

Examples to hear the
difference:
   wear/where*
   witch/which*

*In rapid speech, the initial
"h" sound is often dropped
by even native speakers; but
the students must understand
the dictionary entry.

DO NOT DISTRIBUTE THIS CHART! With chart in hand, some students feel they have a magic solution and so do not work as hard as they otherwise might.

BEGIN WITH A VOLUNTEER, IF YOU HAVE ONE. OTHERWISE CHOOSE ONE OF THE BEST STUDENTS, TO HELP SET A HIGH STANDARD FOR THE CLASS. TO PUT THE STUDENT AT EASE:

LISTEN TO THE STUDENT'S OWN PREFERENCE AND DO IT HIS WAY. IF ANYONE PREFERS TO READ ALONE BUT IS HESITANT, YOU SHOULD SUPPLY A FEW COACHING SOUNDS WHEREVER NEEDED. **IF YOU COACH DURING THE FIRST RECITATION,** THEN ASK THE SAME STUDENT TO REPEAT THE SAME DRILL UNASSISTED BEFORE CONTINUING WITH THE NEXT STUDENT.

DRILL EVERYONE IN YOUR CLASS INDIVIDUALLY IN THE SAME WAY BEFORE CONSIDERING THIS EXERCISE COMPLETED. COMPLIMENT EACH PERSON.

SOUNDS SHOULD BE QUITE ACCURATE, ALTHOUGH NOT NECESSARILY PERFECT AT THIS TIME. IF ANY INDIVIDUAL IS SIGNIFICANTLY BELOW THE CLASS NORM, MAKE A WRITTEN NOTE, AND ASK THAT PERSON TO REMAIN AFTER CLASS. DO NOT EMBARRASS ANYONE WITH PUBLIC CRITICISMS.

ALLOW ABOUT 2-3 MINUTES FOR EACH STUDENT TO COMPLETE EACH ROUND OF DRILLS. DEPENDING ON THE SIZE OF YOUR CLASS, ABOUT 30-45 MINUTES WILL HAVE ELAPSED SINCE THE START OF CLASS. IF SO, YOU ARE ON SCHEDULE. TO THE GROUP:

USING THE SAME TUTOR'S BASIC DRILL CHART, CONDUCT ANOTHER GROUP DRILL. THIS TIME, SKIP AROUND THE CHART AT RANDOM. FORCE THE STUDENTS TO RELY ON THEIR EARS, NOT ON AN EXPECTED PROGRESSION OF WORDS OR SOUNDS. MODEL EVERY WORD AT LEAST ONCE, BUT TWICE AROUND IS BETTER. MODEL MULTIPLE REPETITIONS FOR ANY WORD(S) NOT ACCEPTABLY REPEATED BY THE GROUP. PROBLEMS SHOULD BE DISAPPEARING. WHEN SATISFIED, CONTINUE:

You're doing very well as a group. Now let's see whether we can do as well when working individually. Who wants to be brave and give the first demonstration?

Would you like me to pronounce these words with you, or would you like to try it alone?

I'm very pleased with your performance today. Your pronunciation of the key word sounds is far better than it was on the first day. I can hear the improvement already. Soon you will be able to hear the improvement—because your ear is becoming educated. Once your ear is educated, you can learn to pronounce perfectly...from the dictionary!

To show you how much you have learned, let's do a speed drill. Repeat after me:

Notes: Tasks:

**HOLD UP THE SELECTED DICTIONARY FOR THE CLASS
TO SEE.**

Now you have developed a feeling for the correct pronunciation of the basic sounds of English. These sounds will remain constant for every word you learn from this dictionary—60,000 words!

Almost all the words you will need for daily life are contained in this dictionary.

As I told you last time, we will learn one code among many. Each publisher of a dictionary uses a slightly different code...but the sounds are the same. That is, if our dictionary uses the word "cat" to model that particular sound of the letter "A", another dictionary might use "hat" or "sat."

Beginning next week, we will learn multiple words with the same sounds. Then you will be able to use any brand of dictionary, when necessary.

Also keep in mind that we have learned a basic selection of the most important sounds. However, teachers of speech or linguistics courses sometimes use a diacritical code of fifty or more sounds. They are interested in very subtle differences of sound. A linguist might tell me that I am not using the precise sound expected in a certain word, and I could make a tiny change in pronunciation. But that type of precision is for academic purposes only.

In general, my pronunciation is similar to that used on national radio and television news broadcasts. It is called "standard" English. That's what you are now learning. It is permanently useful to you.

Notes: Tasks:

DISTRIBUTE THE LOANER COPIES OF THE SELECTED DICTIONARY. TWO STUDENTS CAN SHARE, BUT ALL STUDENTS MUST HAVE ACCESS TO A COPY THROUGHOUT THE COURSE.

CONDUCT A PRONUNCIATION EXERCISE, USING ALL THE WORDS IN THE DICTIONARY PRONUNCIATION KEY. MODEL EACH WORD FOR THE STUDENTS TO IMITATE. DURING THE FIRST RUN THROUGH THE CHART, REQUIRE THE SOUNDS TO BE FAIRLY ACCURATE, AND CORRECT THE GROUP AS NEEDED. FOR THE REPEAT RUN, WORK MORE QUICKLY, AND EXPECT THEM TO BE ACCURATE.

CONDUCT A RAPID GROUP DRILL, COVERING EACH KEY WORD AT LEAST ONCE. SINCE THIS BRIEF KEY REPEATS WORDS USED IN THE MAIN KEY, THE SOUNDS SHOULD BE QUITE ACCURATE.

BEGIN WITH A VOLUNTEER. THE STUDENT SHOULD BE ABLE TO REPRODUCE ALL SOUNDS QUITE ACCURATELY. IF YOU HEAR AN ERROR, SUPPLY THE CORRECT SOUND. **DO NOT MODEL ALL THE WORDS, SINCE THIS IS A GAUGE OF MEMORY, NOT IMITATION.** MEMORY IS THE KEY TO SELF-SUFFICIENCY IN THE FUTURE: SOUNDS ARE MORE EASILY PERFECTED IN CLASS.

DRILL ALL STUDENTS BEFORE CONTINUING.

TEXTBOOK FAMILIARIZATION

For our course, I have selected the _____ _____ Dictionary. The Pronunciation Key is located at the front of the book, page _____. Please turn to that page now and repeat the key words after me.

Very good. You'll soon be perfect!
Our dictionary also has a brief version of this Pronunciation Key. The vowel sounds and the voiced diphthongs are located at the foot of the page.
Let's review that key, because you will use it each time you use this dictionary.

Again, the group is performing very well. Who is willing to begin the individual drill on the brief key?

The pronunciation of every word in this dictionary is based on the words and diacritical marks we have just reviewed. As you have just proved to yourselves, these are the same sounds we have already learned.
Now that your sounds are nearing perfection, we can concentrate on pronouncing words with multiple syllables.
Open your dictionary to any page. Notice that the words appear twice. The first entry gives the correct spelling of the word, but that spelling is separated into distinct syllables with the use of hyphens. We learned both of these words last time.

Notes: Tasks:

```
┌─────────────────────────────┐
│ PRINT:                      │
│  hyphen                     │
│  syllable                   │
│                             │
└─────────────────────────────┘
```

```
┌─────────────────────────────┐
│ ADD:                        │
│  syl-la-ble                 │
└─────────────────────────────┘
```

```
┌─────────────────────────────┐
│ ADD:                        │
│  (sĭl-ə-bəl)                │
└─────────────────────────────┘
```

PRONOUNCE EACH SYLLABLE SEPARATELY, AND POINT TO IT AS YOU SAY IT. THEN REPEAT, AT A FASTER RATE, WITH THE STUDENTS IMITATING. THEN SAY IT A THIRD TIME AT NORMAL SPEAKING RATE.

USE THIS PATTERN (SLOW/FASTER/NORMAL) FOR ALL SIMILAR EXAMPLES FOLLOWING. STUDENTS WILL LEARN TO "CONSTRUCT" MULTI-SYLLABIC WORDS THIS WAY.

```
┌──────────────────────────────────────┐
│ PRINT:                               │
│  Stress marks                        │
│  Primary              Secondary      │
│      ˈ                     ˈ          │
│              or                      │
│      ˌ                     ˮ          │
└──────────────────────────────────────┘
```

```
┌─────────────────────────────┐
│ ADD:                        │
│  (sĭl ˈə-bəl)               │
└─────────────────────────────┘
```
Stress mark replaces first hyphen.

Syllables are groups of letters pronounced together. Each syllable has only one vowel sound. That vowel sound could stand alone or could be combined with a consonant. Spelling is not a clue. Find the word "syllable" in your dictionary.

The word "syllable" has three syllables.

In parentheses, you see the correct pronunciation for each of those three syllables. Say "sĭl-ə-bəl."

Any word that has two or more syllables has one primary stress. It could also have one or more secondary stresses, depending on the length of the word.

Therefore, in addition to the hyphens, we also use stress marks. They look like this:

Our dictionary uses a heavy stroke for the primary stress and a light stroke for the secondary stress, if there is one.

Some dictionaries use one heavy stroke for the primary stress plus a pair of lighter strokes for the secondary stress. Both forms are very common. They have exactly the same effect.

Now let's see how stress affects words.

In this word, the primary stress falls on the first syllable. Therefore we emphasize the first syllable. Say "Syllable." (ALL REPEAT)

Notice that the stress mark has *replaced* the hyphen as a separator of the first and second syllables. Only one marker is necessary.

The word "syllable" is a noun. But there are other nouns and verbs that are derived from the same root. Usually such a change of form creates a change in the placement of the stress.

Notes: Tasks:

> PRINT:
> syllabify -verb
> (sĭ-lăb'ə-fī)

> PRINT:
> syllabicate -verb
> syl-lab-i-cate
> (sĭl-lăb' ĭ-kāt")

> PRINT:
> syllabication -noun
> syl-lab-i-ca-tion
> (sĭl-lăb" ĭ-kā'shən)

NOTE: If your selected dictionary shows a slight variation, use that variation to avoid confusion. Also verify all other examples given in this position throughout the course.

> PRINT: television
> ADD: tel-e-vi-sion
> (tĕl-ə-vĭzh-ən)

POINT TO FOUR DISTINCT SYLLABLES ABOVE AS YOU PRONOUNCE EACH.

Because of the changes in spelling, the other words appear above the word we are considering. Spelling, not grammar, determines placement.

When we mark the syllables, we say we "syllabify."

Notice that the stress has shifted. Say "syllabify." (ALL REPEAT)

Notice that another verb is given, with the same meaning. It is the root of still another noun.

The dictionary uses hyphens and stresses to syllabicate the individual words. Say "Syllabicate." (ALL REPEAT)

When a multi-syllable word changes in usage from noun to verb form, often the stresses will change, too.

Say "syllabication." (ALL REPEAT)

You have probably noticed that the pronounced form (shown in parentheses) sometimes is shown with different letters.

That happens because, as I stated earlier, the look of English and the sound of English are different in many words.

Now you know why the most important rule of our class is this slogan:

"Speak English with your ears, not with your eyes!"

Tutors and native speakers of English can help you with pronunciation, of course...yet we're not always nearby when you need us.

So become friends with your dictionary. It is the one dependable source for correct pronunciation that is always available and always correct.

For our next example, let's use a very familiar word—television. Watch how we structure the sounds so that we pronounce the entire word correctly.

Notice that we break it one way to syllabicate it in writing, but we break it differently to say it. Say "tel-ə-vizh-ən." Notice the "zh" ligature.

Notes:

Tasks:

ADD A STRESS MARK: '

(to the "tel" syllable)

ADD SECONDARY
STRESS MARKS: ' or ".

TEACH BOTH THE THICK/THIN & SINGLE/DOUBLE PAIRS BECAUSE BOTH ARE COMMON. **ERASE THE REPLACED HYPHENS.**

PRINT: (whatever is
your text version):
tĕl'ə-vĭzh"ən or
_____ __ _____ ___

TEXT PAGE #:_____.

ALL PUPILS MUST SEE MARKS.

CONDUCT CLASS EXERCISE. LISTEN FOR CORRECT SOUNDS AND STRESSES. WHEN SATISFIED, CONTINUE.

Notice that we emphasize two of the syllables. The heaviest emphasis is on the first syllable: "tel."

So we add a primary (or heavy) stress mark after the first syllable. The weaker emphasis falls on the third syllable; so we add a secondary stress mark.

Our textbook uses _____. Because single and double strokes are easier to see, we will use it here in our class. But be sure you are aware of both forms.

Notice also that the stress mark appears instead of a hyphen only, and so the phonetic rendering of the word "television" looks like this in our text. (PRINT)

Now let's look at the text, to find "television."

Notice the correct spelling with the written syllables separated by hyphens. Then notice the change as the spelled version is converted into the spoken syllable. Place your spoken stresses as marked, and you have perfect pronunciation. Say "television." (ALL REPEAT)

Notes: Tasks:

OPTION:

NOTE: Plural forms of nouns and verbs are not strictly a "dictionary" skill or a sound-production problem, since only three key sounds are involved, the "S," "Z," and final syllable "-ez" for the -es or -ses endings.

However, when reading, students will often chance upon plural forms of new words that cannot be found in the abridged dictionary, which prints only the irregular forms of plurals.

Therefore, by familiarizing students with the basic rules of plural forms, we can enhance their chances of (a) locating the word in its singular form despite irregular endings, and (b) apply the properly spelled plural endings when writing.

Basic information on plural forms is given in Appendix B, together with needed script for leading a ten minute quick familiarization session.

IF YOU SELECT THIS OPTION:

GET AN ANSWER. IF ABOUT HALF OR MORE HAVE THE PROBLEM, CONDUCT THE APPENDIX MATERIAL NOW. IF ONLY A FEW NEED HELP, ASK THOSE INDIVIDUALS TO REMAIN AFTER CLASS.

How many of you have experienced difficulty in forming the plural of nouns and verbs?

Then this is what we will do: _____

_____ .

Notes: Tasks:

NOTE: SELECT APPROPRIATE RESPONSE

CLASS EXERCISE: BEGIN WITH THE VOLUNTEERED WORD. PRINT IT ON THE BLACKBOARD. THEN

OFFER CHALK. ENTER THE SAME WORD'S DICTIONARY PHONETIC CODE UNDER THE CORRECT SPELLING.

POINT OUT CODES IN DICTIONARY LEGEND.

PRONOUNCE SLOWLY AND CAREFULLY. ALL REPEAT. **SAY IT AGAIN, FASTER.** ALL REPEAT. **SAY IT RAPIDLY.** ALL REPEAT. WHEN SATISFIED:

PRINT THE WORD ON THE BOARD.

VERIFY ACCURACY.

ENCOURAGE STUDENTS TO COMPARE NEEDED WORD TO PAGE KEY WORDS.

PRACTICAL APPLICATION

You'll be glad to know we have finished with the study of the *theory* of pronunciation. You need not take any more notes today unless you wish to. However, you should save all your notes, because we will review the key sounds every session, just to be sure our ears stay in perfect tune with the language.

Last time, I asked you to bring a list of problem words. Did you remember to do that? (GET RESPONSE.)

(IF YES:) Very good. You're really trying to learn the English language, and I appreciate that.

(IF NO:) You cannot master the English language unless you make an effort. I will expect you to be fully prepared for class in the future.

Now, let's continue the exercise. Who has a word for us to work on? Do not say it—just spell it.

Find that word in the dictionary. What page is it on? Tell the class. . .(GET RESPONSE.)

All right. Mr/Ms _____, since it is your problem word, please write the pronunciation code as it appears in your dictionary.

Now let's sound it out. The individual vowel sounds are "____, ____, ____," etc. (USE CORRECT PRONUNCIATION CODE.)

Notice how the sounds are marked in the legend. . .

Now say all the syllables slowly, with stresses.

Who has another word? Any volunteers? (GET RESPONSE.) Spell it for me, please.

Everyone look for it in the dictionary. What page? All right, Mr/Ms _____, please come to the blackboard and print both the syllabication and the pronunciation.

Let's sound it out again, exactly as before. The vowel sounds are: ____, ____, ____, etc. (INCLUDE ALL DIPHTHONGS AND LIGATURES IN THE PRACTICE DRILLS.)

Now put the word together, with stresses on the proper syllable. (PRONOUNCE THE WORD CAREFULLY, SLOWLY.)

Now say it at normal speaking speed. (MODEL IT. LISTEN. CORRECT IF NECESSARY. OTHERWISE, COMPLIMENT.)

To complete this exercise, I'd like everyone else to find a problem word in the dictionary, and then be prepared to print it on the blackboard in all three forms. Then we'll all pronounce it together. One or two minutes should be long enough. Find your word. . .write down the page number so we can follow.

Notes: Tasks:

GROUP EXERCISE: WAIT FOR MOST TO FINISH. WHEN READY, ASK TO **HAVE ALL WORDS PRINTED ON THE BLACKBOARD** SIMULTANEOUSLY (OR ON CHART PADS USING FELT PENS), TO SAVE TIME. CALL FOR THE CORRECT SPELLING, THE SYLLABIFIED FORMS, AND THE PHONETIC CODED FORM.

MODEL THE SPOKEN WORDS CORRECTLY FOR THE CLASS TO IMITATE, EVEN IF INCORRECTLY MARKED, TO PREVENT NEGATIVE LEARNING. USE THIS FORM:

VERIFY ACCURACY. IF WRONG, CORRECT ON BLACKBOARD. IF ACCURATE, CONDUCT INDIVIDUAL EXERCISES.

LISTEN. CORRECT AND/OR COMPLIMENT HIM/HER. THEN MODEL THE CORRECT SOUND FOR THE STUDENT TO REPEAT. THEN MODEL IT FOR THE CLASS TO REPEAT. AFTER ALL WORDS HAVE BEEN COVERED:

TAKE AS MANY OTHER WORDS AS TIME PERMITS. THE BALANCE OF THIS SESSION TAKES ONLY 15 MINUTES.

TUTOR: Class, are all the diacritical marks accurate?

Mr/Ms _____, let's you and I pronounce all the syllables, slowly.
(FOLLOW PUPIL'S LEAD: COACH RATHER THAN PROVIDE THE CORRECT SOUNDS.)
Now try to say the word at normal speaking speed. Do you want to try it alone?

You have done something very important: you have converted printed diacritical codes to spoken sounds. Of course it wasn't perfect—perfection takes time. But you have proved that you can do it. This is the basic skill needed for you to master English, and we will practice during each session until it becomes easy.

Notes: <u>Tasks:</u>

```
┌─────────────────────┐
│ PRINT:              │
│  "attribute"        │
└─────────────────────┘
```

```
┌──────────────────────────────────────┐
│ PRINT: (VERIFY IN YOUR TEXT.)         │
│  noun = ăt′rə-byo͞ot″                  │
│  verb = ə-trĭb′ yo͞ot                  │
└──────────────────────────────────────┘
```

```
┌──────────────────────────────────────┐
│ PRINT: (VERIFY IN YOUR TEXT.)         │
│  syllab = at″tri-bu′ tion             │
│  pron = ăt″rə-byo͞o′shən               │
└──────────────────────────────────────┘
```

```
┌──────────────────────────────┐
│ PRINT: gravely               │
│  grave = serious             │
│  gravel = small stones       │
└──────────────────────────────┘
```

```
┌──────────────────────────┐
│ PRINT: "fix"             │
└──────────────────────────┘
```

NOTE: If using different dictionary, check entry. Adjust comments to suit, if necessary.

MULTIPLE ENTRIES

You now know the secret for pronouncing all words.

But before we finish for today, I want to be sure you understand that syllabication and stresses change within the same word as we add an ending—or sometimes when we change from the noun to the verb meaning.

Consider this word. (DO **NOT** SAY IT.)

This word can be pronounced in two ways, depending on whether it is used as a noun or a verb. If it is a noun, we do this:

In the noun, we accent the first and last syllables. Say *ăt'rə-byōot".* (ALL REPEAT.)

In the verb form, we have only one accent—the middle syllable. Say *ə-trib'byōo̅t.* (ALL REPEAT.)

Now, watch the stresses change if we add a "-tion" ending to the noun form.

Say *at"rə-bū'shən.* (ALL REPEAT, SEVERAL TIMES, IF NECESSARY.)

Keep in mind that even when you already pronounce the root word correctly, *a change in ending or usage could change the stresses considerably.*

Sometimes, a change in endings will make two very different words look the same. Then we must understand from the context which word is intended.

This word, too, has two distinct pronunciations. So you must know whether you are talking about something very serious, "grāve-ly," or something stoney, "grav-el-ly."

The word "grave" is curious because it has three distinct meanings, all, different parts of speech. Therefore there are three separate entries in our dictionary. These meanings are numbered, as a signal. Look for the word "grave" on page _____.

Do you see how the three different usages are indicated? (ANSWER ANY QUESTIONS.)

However, some words have a number of related meanings or uses. Then the dictionary might use numbers or letters to distinguish usages. Find the word "fix" in your dictionary.

Notes: Tasks:

```
┌─────────────────────────────┐
│ PRINT:                      │
│   the record/to record      │
│   the im'print/to imprint'  │
└─────────────────────────────┘
```

IF HALF OR MORE OF THE STUDENTS HAVE PROBLEMS, OFFER TO CONDUCT A SPECIAL EXERCISE RELATING TO THE TRANSIT SYSTEM AND MAPS. BE PREPARED TO PROVIDE TWO OR MORE MAPS NEXT TIME.

COLLECT LOANER DICTIONARIES

PURPOSE: THE PURPOSE OF THIS SESSION IS TO CONVERT THE THEORY AND SPECIFIC SOUNDS LEARNED IN THE FIRST SESSION INTO PRACTICAL ABILITY IN THIS SESSION. ALL STUDENTS SHOULD BE EXPECTED TO PROVE THEIR ABILITY TO MAKE THE CONVERSION FROM PHONETIC CODES INTO FAIRLY ACCURATE ENGLISH SOUNDS. DO NOT DEMAND OR EXPECT PERFECTION, BUT BE PREPARED TO REWARD A PERFECT RESPONSE WITH PRAISE, IF IT OCCURS.

IF YOU DO NOT UNDERSTAND THAT PURPOSE CLEARLY, GO BACK AND RE-READ THIS ENTIRE SESSION.

Notice that the main entry is shown as a verb, with ten variations of meaning. Then an informal usage is indicated. Then the noun meaning is given, although *not* with a separate entry for its four key variations, including slang. Our dictionary is not consistent, and I don't know why. Simply be aware that you should check for additional entries each time.

When you check the entries above and below the given word, you will be more certain that you are using the correct pronunciation for the particular meaning you have in mind.

Although the pronunciation does not change for the words "grave" or "fix," pronunciation does change with meaning for other words, as we have already seen. This is especially true of two-syllable noun/verb words.

To be safe, always check your dictionary.

In addition, I would like you to use only an American-English dictionary for pronunciation. Some of you already have foreign editions of dictionaries, and many of those editions use British-English, as well as different code systems.

If you already own a foreign edition of a bilingual dictionary, please use it only to translate foreign words into English. Then find the pronunciation in the American-English dictionary. I realize that this is bothersome, but I think it is necessary.

You are doing very well as a class. Now that you understand the diacritical codes and how they are used, you need to practice the sounds so that you develop a good command of them. That will take time, of course, but we still have many more practice hours in this course.

In the next few sessions, we will concentrate our group efforts in three areas: normal conversation, pretend telephone calls to other class members, and reading aloud.

That variety of practice will give you real confidence in your ability to speak English correctly.

Is everyone familiar with the public transportation system? (YES/NO) Do you have problems getting the right information by telephone? (YES/NO).

I'll bring materials needed for telephone calls next time. You bring your notes for quick review.

Until next _____-day at _____ am/pm...goodbye.

END

THIRD SESSION

THIRD SESSION

Notes: Tasks:

DURING YOUR PRELIMINARY, PRE-CLASS STUDY OF THIS TUTORING SESSION, LIST MATERIALS NEEDED FOR THE CLASS HERE:

PREPARE TO REVIEW THESE DRILL MATERIALS: TUTOR'S BASIC DRILL CHART, DICTIONARY PRONUNCIATION KEY, AND THE VOCABULARY DRILL CHART, FOLLOWING.

PLAN TO DRILL THE GROUP AS WELL AS INDIVIDUALS. INDIVIDUAL WORK IS AN EXERCISE, NOT A "TEST." STUDENTS SHOULD DEPEND ON THEIR EARS FOR ACCURACY. THE LESSON PLAN THEN SLIDES THROUGH A SYLLABIFICATION REVIEW INTO THE CONVERSATIONAL-ENGLISH EXERCISES.

CONDUCT AN EXERCISE AT NORMAL SPEAKING RATES, USING THE TUTOR'S BASIC DRILL CHART. DRILL THE KEY WORDS ONLY, NOT THE DIACRITICAL MARKS AS SUCH. COVER ALL CATEGORIES. BE MORE DEMANDING THAN IN PREVIOUS SESSIONS: THE STUDENTS' SOUNDS SHOULD BE APPROACHING PERFECTION (FOR THE EASIER VOWEL SOUNDS) AND QUITE ACCEPTABLE (FOR THE MORE DIFFICULT SOUNDS, INCLUDING "R").

WHEN THE GROUP IS ABLE TO MAKE ALL SOUNDS ACCEPTABLY (POSSIBLY EXCEPTING "R"), CONSIDER THIS DRILL COMPLETED AND GO ON TO THE NEXT.

IF YOU HEAR NUMEROUS ERRORS, DRILL INDIVIDUALS ON THE SAME MATERIAL, COACHING THE CORRECT SOUNDS AS NEEDED, AND NOTING THE NAMES OF INDIVIDUALS WHO NEED ADDITIONAL HELP. ASK THEM TO REMAIN AFTER CLASS.

WHEN THE SOUNDS ARE ACCEPTABLE FROM MOST OF THE CLASS, CONTINUE:

THIRD SESSION

◄——— *DURING ADVANCE PREPARATION, DO THIS*

TUTOR: Today we are going to see how fast your ears are working. We will drill with the key sounds already learned, and we will depend on our ears alone to guide us to the correct sounds. Do not use your notes. Just listen and repeat after me:

P R A C T I C A L   W O R D   P O W E R

TUTOR'S BASIC DRILL CHART*

Symbols:	A	E	I	O	U
ˉ = bar	ā = late	ē = see	ī = tie	ō = go	ū = use
˘ = arc	ă = cat	ĕ = ten	ĭ = sit	ŏ = hot	= yo͞o
ˆ = tent	â = care	er = ûr	î = pier	ô = for,	ŭ = mud
¨ = dots	ä = father	(stressed)	ir = ûr	fought	û = urge
		er = ər	(stressed)	or = ûr	ûr = term
		(unstressed)	i = ē	(word)	sir
			(ski = skē)		word
					heard

Y	Schwa: ə and ər	R
y = yes	thə (book)	Do not drill prior to
y = ī (sky)	thē (apple)	instruction in Second and
y = ē (fairly)	ər = doctor, baker,	Third Sessions. (see
and in most "ly"	murmur	Appendix A) Sound is "are"
adverbial endings	Sometimes: apostrophe =	
	ə + l,m,n,r	
	(in unstressed syllables;	
	see Appendix A)	

Diphthongs: (International code with English spelling equivalents)

oi	au	ai
oi = oil	ou = out, count	ai = ī
boy	how, cow	Thailand
	tower, towel	kaiser

* **NOTE:** Be sure to correct all deficiencies in
sound production. See Appendix A.

(continued on next page)

DO NOT DISTRIBUTE THIS CHART! With chart in hand, some students feel they have a magic solution and so do not work as hard as they otherwise might.

PRACTICAL WORD POWER

TUTOR'S BASIC DRILL CHART, continued

Voiced/Voiceless Pairs:

1. **explosives:**
   - t/d = time/dime
   - p/b = pin/bin
   - k/g = kilt/guilt

2. **sibilants:**
   - s/z = so/zone
   - sh/zh = cash/casual
   - ch/j = cherry/Jerry

3. **others:**
   - f/v = ferry/very
   - th/**th** = bath/bathing

4. **relationships:**
   - exploded- sh = ch
   - exploded- zh = j

"eng" Sounds:
See Appendix A

- "eng" = ng ligature
  - = ŋ symbol
- -ng = sing, sang
  - song, sung
  - length
- -ng-ng = singing
  - bringing
- -ng + k = ink, thank
- -ng + g = finger, anger

(Memory hook: "NG" in dictionary means "No G.")

Other tricky letters and sounds:

Unsure letters:

G:
- spelling "g" = gum, gem, beige
- dictionary "g" = go, gum **only**.

C:
- c = s = place
- c = k = cup
- c = ch = cello
- cc = ks = success
- cc = k = accord

X:
- x = ks = extra, Mexico Texas
- x = gz = exit
- x = z = xylophone

Q:
- qu = kw = quick, quality
- qu = k = quiche, quay
- qu + = k = discotheque communiquè

F:
ph or gh = f (printed)
photograph, phase, phone
laugh, tough, enough
Philadelphia

Disappearing letters:
- often = of'ən
- know = nō
- hour = our
- walk = wôk
- bomb = bäm
- time = tīm
- who = ho͞o
- answer = an'sər

Note: there are many other words students will know; some are reviewed in the Third Session.

Letter "H" behaviors:

- —disappears = Thomas ghost
- —begins = have help
- —replaces = who = ho͞o
- —precedes = which = hwĭch*

Examples to hear the difference:
wear/where*
witch/which*

*In rapid speech, the initial "h" sound is often dropped by even native speakers; but the students must understand the dictionary entry.

DO NOT DISTRIBUTE THIS CHART! With chart in hand, some students feel they have a magic solution and so do not work as hard as they otherwise might.

DRILL THE GROUP ON THE DICTIONARY KEY. OPTION: IF ALL THE STUDENTS PERFORMED EXCEPTIONALLY WELL ON THE PRECEDING DRILL, USE THE BRIEF KEY AT THE FOOT OF THE PAGES. IF ABOUT HALF OF THE GROUP ARE STILL HAVING PROBLEMS WITH SOUNDS OTHER THAN "R", THEN USE THE MAIN KEY AT THE FRONT OF THE BOOK, AND DRILL INDIVIDUALS AFTER THE GROUP FINISHES.

CONDUCT A DRILL WITH NEW WORDS, USING THE "VOCABULARY DRILL CHART" FOLLOWING. COMPLETE AN ENTIRE DRILL SEQUENCE WITH THE GROUP, USING AT LEAST THREE OF THE WORDS LISTED UNDER EACH OF THE DIACRITICAL CODE MARKS.

ALTHOUGH THE WORDS ARE NEW, THE SOUNDS ARE NOT. THEREFORE, STUDENTS SHOULD BE IMITATING YOUR MODEL SOUND WITH THE SAME ACCURACY AS SHOWN ON THE PRECEDING DRILLS. THEREFORE, YOU SHOULD CORRECT ANY ERRORS BY REPEATING THE GIVEN WORD(S) UNTIL YOU HEAR ACCURATE SOUNDS. AS BEFORE, THE GROUP NORM SHOULD BE NEARING PERFECTION, WITH THE POSSIBLE EXCEPTION OF THE "R" SOUNDS.

I am really pleased with your progress in forming the correct sounds of English. Now let's see whether you can do as well with the dictionary Pronunciation Key.

Your ears are beginning to work very well in cooperation with your tongue. I think you are now ready to try new words. I'll pronounce the new words, and you repeat them. Let's work as quickly as possible, so that your ear learns to respond to the speed of normal conversation.

PRACTICAL WORD POWER

VOCABULARY DRILL CHART

A

ā — late	ă — cat	â — care	ä — father
ate	at	pare	alms
age	act	scare	calm
day	hat	dare	palm
state	can	marry	mama
pray	class	carry	arm
name	glass	prayer	car
play	black	Mary	far
table	fast	stare	part
case	mad	*	barter
cake	glad	Crazies:	barley
able	grasp	there	are
*	match	where	Argentina
Crazies:	apple	air	*
weigh	ask	pair	Crazies:
eight	France	chair	heart
aim	*	stairs	hearth
faint	Crazies:	merry	bomb
maid	laugh	err	
steak	plaid	heir	
break		Puerto Rico	
vein		Arizona	
buffet		wear	
gauge			
they			
neighbor			
Spain			

E

ē — see	ĕ — ten	er = ur	er = ər
be/bee	pen	In stressed syllables; see ûr.	In unstressed syllables; see ər.
he/she	pet		
free	bet		
seem	bed		
feel	red		
green	edge		
beef	ever		
feet	every		
agree	exit		
Greece	end		
Sweden	*		
*	Crazies:		
Crazies:	said		
read	any		
please	friend		
east	says		
easy	guess		
tea	leopard		
eat	berry		
meat	ferry		
steal	bury		
quay	steady		
people	ready		
seize	pleasure		
believe			
thief			
suite			
field			
police			
ceiling			
receive			

I

ī — tie	ĭ — sit	î — pier	ir = ûr	i = ē
I	it	pirouette	In stressed syllables; see ûr.	ski
ice	is	nirvana		visa
idea	in	*		medium
pie	hit	Crazies:		mediate
like	did	ear		police
file	ill	hear		
white	thick	hero		
rise	thin	steer		
fine	lip	beer		
knife	ship	dear		
ivory	winter	clear		
high	inch	weird		
island	if	cheer		
child	Italy	peer		
Friday	India	fear		
China	milk			
*	mid-			
Crazies:	*			
buy	Crazies:			
by	pretty			
island	build			
eye	built			
why	sieve			
aisle	business			
high	women			
thyme	children			
style	gypsy			
cry	gym			
try	system			
fly				

PRACTICAL WORD POWER

VOCABULARY DRILL CHART, continued

O				U			Y	"schwa" vowel
ō	ŏ	ô	or	ū = yōō	ŭ	û	y (printed) =	ə and ər
go	hot	for	= ûr	use	mud	urge	yes, yet	the (book)
oh	on	ought	In stressed syllables; see ûr.	fuse	fun	fur	yesterday	ago
toe	fond	or/ore		cute	run	hurt	yellow	above
hold	pond	more		accuse	but	murder	yield	about
post	lock	born		value	bus	further	yard	again
rose	lot	worn		fuel	cup	burn	yawn	
lone	olive	off		cure	just	sturdy	yours	ALSO:
cold	odd	fought		pure	dumb	hurry	beyond	vowel + r
gold	October	ought		humor	study	urgent		(in unstressed
joke		thought		huge	sum	urn	ALSO:	syllables):
flow		cost		union	thunder	urban	all ū or yōō	baker
folk		glory		unique	summer	Turkey	words.	teacher
old		Florida			under			doctor
Bolivia		Korea		*	ugly	*	ALSO:	dollar
		Portugal		Crazies:	Russia	Crazies:	y = i (printed)	murmur
*		Norway		you		earn	sky	error
				few	*	learn	fly	
Crazies:		*		beauty	Crazies:	bird	try	ALSO: shown in
dough		Crazies:		news	flood	first	deny	most "-tion" endings,
loaf		all		Europe	blood	third	rye	pronounced "shən"
sew		awe		Yule	front	word	awry	
beau		war		youth	done	world	apply	ALSO: printed as
plateau		floor		jewel	come	worm		an apostrophe before
owe		door		yew	some	earth	ALSO:	unstressed consonants
bowl		law		ewe	money	thorough	y = e (printed)	in some dictionaries.
although		paw		your	dozen	birth	ready	
brooch		straw		yours	mother	perk	steady	
yeoman		draw			of	stern	belly	
soul		caught			oven	were	jelly	
		court			does	early	silly	
		course			onion	certain		
		coarse			Monday	effort	plus most adverbial	
		doll			country	Germany	"-ly" endings:	
		ball			shovel		fairly	
		dog					easily	
							slowly	
							quickly	

© 1989, 1987 by Richard Cavalier

PRACTICAL WORD POWER

VOCABULARY DRILL CHART, continued

Diphthongs

oi = oi (printed):
oil, boy, boil, foil, toilet
point, joint, coin
spoil, Illinois

—spelled "oy"
boy, toy, ploy
royal, destroy

au = ou (printed):

—spelled "ou"
out, about, count, county
boundary, found, round
south, pound, astound, cloud
drought, bounce

—spelled "ow"
how, cow, now, down
power, owl, tower, towel
plow, shower, flower

ai = ī (printed):
Thailand, kaiser
Shanghai, Hawaii

"oo" Ligature

oo = o͝o (printed):
foot, book, took, look
shook, soot, could, would
poor, should, woman

oo = o͞o (printed):
food, cool, fool, dew, tool
school, blue, clue, soothe
shoe, fruit, through, prove
neutral, tomb, do, to

ū = yo͞o (printed):
cute, fuel, you, beauty, feud
few, fumes, Cuba, Yugoslavia

Spelling exceptions:

oo = ô (printed):
door, floor

oo = ŭ (printed):
flood, blood

Voiced/Unvoiced Consonants and Ligatures:

f/v:
ferry/very
fast/vast
feel/veal

s/z:
so/zone
sip/zip
seal/zeal

t/d:
time/dime
plant/planned
to/do

sh/zh:
shoe, shirt, push, sure
sugar, cash, dish, wish
shampoo, show

beige, garage, casual
azure, pleasure, leisure
Baton Rouge

p/b:
pin/bin
cap/cab
pill/bill

"sh" variants:
mission, passion, machine
Chicago, special, appreciate
nation, ratio

k/g:
kilt/guilt
tack/tag
hawk/hog

ch/j:
choke/joke
cherry/Jerry

cheese, children, lunch
check, bench, China, Chile
chapter, challenge, choice

th/th:

th:
bath, teeth, cloth, thick
thin, think, thirty, tenth
thousand, north, south
Thursday

th:
these, those, that, this
the, bathing, clothing
northern, southern, father
mother, brother
Netherlands

jump, just, jewel, major
January, joy, jade, jail
Japan, junior, jelly

"j" variants:
edge, pledge, judge
educate, adulation
gem, gin, gym, agitate

© 1989, 1987 by Richard Cavalier

PRACTICAL WORD POWER

VOCABULARY DRILL CHART, continued

Other tricky letters and sounds:

"eng" sounds:

"eng" = ng ligature
= ŋ symbol

-ng:
sing, sang, song, sung
length, long, fling, swing
swung, bang, hang, England

-ng-ng = ŋ - ŋ:
singing, bringing, swinging
longing, banging, hanging

-ng + k:
ink, think, blink, brink
bank, thank you, tank
frank, sank, sunk, honk
(uncle, sanction)

-ng + k + -ng:
drinking, thinking
blinking, linking

-ng + g:
finger, anger, hunger
linger, Hungary, Hungarian

Spelling exceptions:
(no "eng")
strange/stranger
plunge/plunger
range/ranger
change/changing
danger/dangerous

Unsure letters:

G:
—spelling "g" = gum, gem, beige
—dictionary "g" = go, gum only

C:
c = s = place, price, ace dice
ice, certain
c = k = cup, cab, captain, capable
cover, cure
c = ch = cello (exception)
cc = ks = success, access, accent
accept, eccentric, Occident
cc = k = accord, account, accomplish
occasion, occupation, occur

X:
x = ks = extra, Mexico, Texas
expense, Oxford, fox
x = gs = exit, exert, exile
exhaust, exhort
x = z = xylophone

Q:
qu = kw = quick, quiet, quality, quota
queen, quorum, question
quiz, quart
(begining)
qu = k = quiche, quay
(ending)
qu + = discotheque, communique
plaque, antique

ph or gh = f (printed):
photograph, phase, phone, laugh, tough
rough, enough, Philadelphia

Disappearing letters:
often
know
hour
walk
talk
bomb
who
which
answer
half

Letter "H" behaviors:
—disappears = Thomas, Thailand
hour, Utah, ghost
—begins = have, hint, help, hope
hum, humor
—replaces = who, whom, whole
wholesome, wholistic
—precedes = which, what, when, where
whether, while, white

Notes: Tasks:

DISTRIBUTE THE VOCABULARY DRILL CHART (VOWEL SOUNDS/DIPHTHONGS/LIGATURES) BY PHOTOCOPYING THE VERSION PRINTED ON THE PRECEDING PAGES.

THERE ARE SEVERAL HUNDRED WORDS ON THIS CHART. DO NOT ATTEMPT TO COVER ALL IN ONE CLASS! JUST DO A FEW FROM EACH COLUMN IN ANY GIVEN EXERCISE PERIOD, CHECKING OFF THE WORDS USED (OR MISPRONOUNCED). CONTINUE WITH NEW WORDS AT THE NEXT DRILL PERIOD.

DRILL THE GROUP BY PRONOUNCING ONLY THE FIRST WORD UNDER EACH DIACRITICAL CODE MARK AS A MODEL. FOR ALL THE OTHER WORDS IN THE COLUMN, STUDENTS SHOULD ACCURATELY SUPPLY THE CORRECT PRONUNCIATION THEMSELVES. LISTEN AND MAKE CORRECTIONS, IF NEEDED.

IF MOST OF THE STUDENTS ARE MAKING MOST OF THE SOUNDS CORRECTLY, COMPLETE THE DRILL AS BEGUN. IF ERRORS ARE FREQUENT, STOP THE PROCESS. BEGIN AGAIN BY SUPPLYING THE CORRECT MODEL WORD AND ALSO BY READING ALL WORDS WITH THE CLASS, AS AN AID. IT SHOULD NOT BE NECESSARY TO MODEL EVERY WORD FOR IMITATION; BUT IF NEEDED, MODEL ONLY A FEW NEW WORDS IN EACH CATEGORY AND SAVE THE BALANCE OF THE CHART FOR FUTURE DRILLS.

ELIMINATING ACCENTS

You have shown an amazing progress in your ability to reproduce the sounds of standard English. Can you hear the difference? (MAYBE.) Soon you will be sure.

Well don't be concerned, because now that you have learned to make the correct sounds, you will learn all new vocabulary without an accent. Also, as you begin to recognize the difference between correct sounds and those you might be using with old vocabulary, you can begin to correct the old words.

Of course we would like to correct the worst of the problems with your old vocabulary, but because of habit, correction will take time.

There is more benefit to learning many new words correctly...more benefit to gaining confidence in your ability to pronounce correctly from the dictionary. When you are comfortable with your dictionary skills, you are in control of 60,000 words, old and new. Then you will be independent in developing new vocabulary.

Let's learn more new words.

If you continue to develop your skills so rapidly, you will be very fluent and very confident before this course is finished.

Now, let's go on to new material.

Last session, we were working on dictionary syllabification and the pronunciation code. Do you remember the word "television"?

Notes: Tasks:

```
┌─────────────────────────────────────┐
│ PRINT:                              │
│  television = spelled               │
│  tel-e-vi-sion = syllabified        │
│  tĕl′ə-vĭzh″ən = pronounced         │
└─────────────────────────────────────┘
```

NOTE: Use your text's code, if different

NOTE: If no one can answer correctly, circle
the "vizh" syllable and review the ideas of
voicing and ligatures.

SYLLABIFICATION

To review: the first form is the correct spelling. The second is the written syllabification. The third form is the spoken syllabification with all the necessary diacritical marks. Notice that we use both primary and secondary stress marks; and that stress marks replace the hyphens in those positions.

Say "television." (ALL REPEAT UNTIL PERFECT.)

Which syllable contains a voiced ligature?

It's very nice to be able to make correct sounds and to pronounce individual words correctly. But the purpose of correct pronunciation is to make daily conversation easier and more productive.

Therefore we will spend the balance of this class learning common phrases that can bring specific answers to questions not everyone knows how to phrase.

Today we'll work with phrases relating to restaurants and entertainment.

(OPTIONAL:) We will also work on getting information relating to public transportation.

Before we begin, do you have any questions on anything we have worked on so far today? (ANSWER FULLY.)

Notes:　　　　　　　　　　　　　　　　　Tasks:

PRINT:
reserve = rĭ-zŭrv´
reservation
res-er-va-tion
(rĕz˝êr-vā´shən)

NOTE: Use your text's code, if different.

1.

PRINT: "Pricing"
cost = kôst
cover = kŭv´ər
minimum = mĭn´ĭ-mŭm
ticket = tĭk´et
charge =chärj

MAKING TELEPHONE CALLS

Nobody likes to sit at home all weekend just because information seems difficult to obtain. In fact, it's easy to get information for almost any purpose, because the telephone is everywhere.

Many public libraries offer free telephone information service. Local and federal government offices offer information and directory service to help you find the proper department to answer your question.

Problems with telephone conversations arise because you cannot see the person you are talking with. Therefore neither person cannot *see* when the other person does not understand. As a result, the problem grows, and so both persons are often eager to end the conversation.

To be sure the telephone is not a handicap, we will make pretend telephone calls to each other. If you turn your chair and face away from your partner, then our classroom situation is just like the telephone situation. You'll see how easy it can be.

Most good restaurants and the most popular stage shows require reservations.

Say "reserve." (ALL REPEAT) Say "reservation." (ALL REPEAT UNTIL ACCURATE.)

When making reservations, or appointments, time is an important consideration. But for entertainment, cost is also an important detail.

Cost can be stated in any of three main ways:

At a fine restaurant, there is probably a cover charge. This is the cost of being seated at the table and does not include the cost of the food and beverages. Everything is extra.

At a nightclub, you might pay a minimum charge. The minimum is the least amount of money you must spend if you go inside. The minimum charge is included in your final bill if you spend more than that stated amount.

At a stage show, or a movie, or a sports event, you will pay for a ticket, and that should be your only cost to enter and view the presentation.

Sometimes you are required to pay both a ticket price and a minimum charge. Very often you will hear the words "door charge", which is the same as a ticket price. You might also be asked to pay a "two-drink minimum", the most commonly stated charge.

<u>Notes:</u>   <u>Tasks:</u>

CONDUCT GROUP EXERCISE: TAKING ONLY ONE PHRASE AT A TIME, PRINT THE ENTIRE "MAKING RESERVATIONS" CHART, FROM THE FOLLOWING PAGES, ON THE BLACKBOARD.

READ EACH INDIVIDUAL PHRASE SLOWLY AND ASK THE GROUP TO IMITATE. THEN REPEAT AT A FASTER RATE AND A THIRD TIME AT A NORMAL SPEAKING RATE. WHEN THE GROUP RESPONSE IS ACCEPTABLY ACCURATE, ASK EACH INDIVIDUAL TO READ ONE PHRASE, WORKING IN ROTATION UNTIL ALL PHRASES HAVE BEEN COVERED AND/OR EACH STUDENT HAS READ AT LEAST TWO PHRASES.

OPTION: YOU CAN ALSO MODEL VARIATIONS ON THESE PHRASES AND DISCUSS THEM CASUALLY, OR YOU CAN USE (AND BLACKBOARD) THE SCRIPTED DISCUSSION ON PAGES FOLLOWING THE CHART. DISTRIBUTE COPIES OF THE RESERVATIONS PHRASES IF YOU CHOOSE THE CASUAL OPTION.

If you don't want to be surprised by the cost, be sure you ask all the appropriate questions. Today we will practice asking and answering some of the most common questions.

Let's begin with these important words.

Say "cost...cover...minimum...ticket...charge". (ALL REPEAT) Say "cover charge...minimum charge...ticket charge." (ALL REPEAT)

Fortunately, many standard phrases are used. It is not necessary that you use these exact words when asking questions, of course. Yet, by learning them, you will be prepared to ask, to answer, and to understand.

Notes: Tasks:

"Practical Word Power"
MAKING RESERVATIONS

(Key terms)

1. Reservation; cost, cover, minimum, ticket...cover charge, minimum charge.

(Restaurant)

2. "Are you still taking reservations for Thanksgiving dinner?"
3. "How many in your party?"
4. "Yes/No. Your name please?"
5. "Is your menu a la carte or prix fixe?" (Pronounced pre-feks = price fixed.)
6. "Main course" often called "entre"
7. "Side dishes"
8. "Can you seat four for dinner at eight o'clock tonight?"

(Movies)

9. "What's playing today?" (Response: title of movie)
10. "What are the show times?" (Response: one or more clock times)
11. "What is the Motion Picture Code for this film?"
     Possible responses:
      G = for general audiences
      PG = parental guidance needed
      R = restricted; under 17 years accompanied by parent
      X = adults only (over 18 years old)
12. "What price are the tickets?"
13. "Do you have plenty of seats now?"
14. "We're sold out for this showing. You can buy tickets now for the next showing, at _____ o'clock."

NOTE: To make an informal presentation, print and discuss these phrases, one at a time. If you prefer to make a scripted presentation, begin reading on page 127. Use these sample phrases, as indicated by the numbers.

Notes: Tasks:

"Practical Word Power"
MAKING RESERVATIONS cont'd

(Theatres and concerts)

15. "Are seats (or tickets) still available for (event)_____?"
16. "On what date?" or "For which date?"
17. "How many seats?...Yes/No."
18. If no: "Which dates are still open?" or "Which performance is still available?"
19. "Sorry, all sold out."
20. If yes: "Which locations and price ranges?" (Response: locations and prices)
21. "I'd like to reserve _____."
22. "Which credit cards do you accept?"
23. "How late will you hold the tickets?"
24. "Until one hour before curtain time."
25. "What is my reservation number (or your name)?"
26. "Where can I park?"
27. "Is it free?" Yes/No (or "Is it reduced rate?")
28. "We'll stamp your ticket." (for reduced rate)

Additional phrases:

_____
_____
_____
_____
_____
_____
_____
_____

<u>Notes:</u>   <u>Tasks:</u>

2.

> PRINT:
> "Are you still taking
> reservations for
> Thanksgiving dinner?"

READ SLOWLY/FASTER/NORMAL

3.

> PRINT: "How many
> in your party?"

4.

> PRINT: "Yes/No.
> Your name, please?"

5.

> PRINT:
> "Is your menu á la
> carte or prix fixe?"
>   ä lä kärt
>   prē-fēks

6.

> PRINT: main course

7.

> PRINT: side dish

Define, if necessary.

MAKING RESERVATIONS

When calling a restaurant, you might ask:

Say "Are you still...taking reservations...for Thanksgiving dinner?" (ALL REPEAT)

The host or hostess will probably answer with a question: "How many (persons or diners or people) in your party?"

The restaurant might be able to seat two or four people, but not ten or twenty. Once you state the number, the answer is either *yes* or *no.* If yes, they will ask for your name.

Say "How many in your party?" (ALL REPEAT)

Say "Yes, we can seat a party of five...Your name, please?"

To understand the pricing system, you can ask:

Say "Is your menu á la carte...or prix fixe?" (ALL REPEAT)

The phrase "a la carte" is French and means "from the card"—or menu. That means you order any dish at the price printed.

The phrase "prix fixe" means "fixed price." It indicates that you choose your

main course, and all the other foods served as *side dishes*

are included in the price stated for the main course.

Notes: Tasks:

8a.

> PRINT:
> "Can you seat a
> party of four"

8b.

> ADD:
> for lunch/dinner at
> ____ o'clock tonight?"

(MOVIES:)

9.

> PRINT:
> What's playing today?

10.

> ADD:
> What are the show times?

11.

> PRINT:
> Motion Picture Code:
> G = general audience
> PG = parental guidance
> R = restricted; under
>   17 years need parent
> X = adults only (over 18)

12.

> PRINT: (Phrase as stated)

13.

> PRINT: (Phrase as stated)

14.

> PRINT: (Phrase as stated)

Here's another way to ask for the same information:

Let's practice. Repeat after me: "Can you seat a party of four. . ." (ALL REPEAT.)

"For dinner at 8 o'clock tonight?" (ALL REPEAT.) Now the entire phrase: "Can you seat a party of four for dinner at 8 o'clock tonight?" (ALL REPEAT UNTIL THE WORDS FLOW EASILY.)

When calling about movies, we ask, "What's playing today?" You'll get the title, in reply, and possibly the names of the stars. If interested, you'll then ask, "What are the show times?" The answer will be the starting hour for each showing.

Let me hear you ask "What's playing today?" (ALL REPEAT.) And "What are the show times?" (ALL REPEAT.)

If you have children, you will also want to ask about the industry code.

Let me hear you ask: "What is the Motion Picture Code for this film?" (ALL REPEAT UNTIL SMOOTH.)

"What price are the tickets?" (ALL REPEAT.)

And you might want to ask: "Do you have plenty of seats now?" The answer could be *yes* or *no;* but it could also be:

"We are sold out for this show." Or "It has started. But you can buy tickets now for the next showing."

Ask me, "What price are the tickets?" (ALL REPEAT.)

"Do you still have plenty of seats?" (ALL REPEAT.)

That's fine. I'm sure you can get into the movies without a problem. Do you have any questions about any of this? (IF SO, ANSWER FULLY.)

Notes: Tasks:

(Theatres & Concerts:)

15.
PRINT: (Phrase as stated)

16.
PRINT: (Phrase as stated)

17.
PRINT: (Phrase as stated)

18.
PRINT: (Phrase as stated)

19.
PRINT: (Phrase as stated)

20.
PRINT: (Phrase as stated)

21.
PRINT: (Phrase as stated)

22.
PRINT: (Phrase as stated)

23.
PRINT: (Phrase as stated)

THEATRES AND CONCERTS

Now let's talk about getting tickets for theatres and concerts, because these transactions have the greatest number of variables...and the greatest chance for mistakes.

When calling, you ask, "Are seats (or tickets) still available for (Event) _____?"

And the response will be, "On what date?" And then, "How many?" Then, yes or no.

If the answer is no, then you ask, "Which dates are still open?" or "Which performance is still available?" It could be, "Sorry—sold out."

Now let's hear all these phrases. First, "Are seats still available for (Event) _____?" (ALL REPEAT.) "Which dates are still open?" (ALL REPEAT.) Or we can say, "Which performance is still available?" (ALL REPEAT UNTIL SATISFACTORY.)

If seats *are available* on an acceptable date, then you have to ask about the price. So then we ask,

"Which locations and price ranges?" And the answer could be main floor, $20; first balcony, $15; and second balcony, $7. Or you could hear, "One price—$15—no reserved seating." Most events for adults are reserved.

But if you're still interested, try to reserve.

"I'd like to reserve five seats at $15. My name is _____." (ALL REPEAT.)

Then money. "Which credit cards do you accept?" Let me hear you say it. (ALL REPEAT.)

Notes: Tasks:

24.

┌─────────────────────────────┐
│ PRINT: (Phrase as stated)   │
└─────────────────────────────┘

┌─────────────────────────────┐
│ PRINT: curtain time   │
└─────────────────────────────┘

25.

┌─────────────────────────────┐
│ PRINT: (Phrase as stated)   │
└─────────────────────────────┘

26.

┌─────────────────────────────┐
│ PRINT: (Phrases as stated) │
└─────────────────────────────┘

27a.

┌─────────────────────────────┐
│ PRINT: (Phrase as stated)   │
└─────────────────────────────┘

27b.

┌─────────────────────────────┐
│ PRINT: (Phrase as stated)   │
└─────────────────────────────┘

28.

┌─────────────────────────────┐
│ PRINT: (Phrase as stated)   │
└─────────────────────────────┘

NOTE: Regardless of whether you have
worked from the script or casually, by
discussion, this exercise is now complete.
Now go on to the Telephone Calls Exercise.

Important information: "How late will you hold the tickets?"

The usual answer is "Until one hour before performance time." A theatre will say, "Until one hour before *curtain* time."

Now, "How late will you hold tickets?" (ALL REPEAT.) Now, "Until one hour before performance time." (REPEAT.)

If you give your credit card number, be sure to get a reservation number or the name of the phone clerk. Otherwise a mix-up could be expensive.

So we ask, "What is my reservation number?" Say it. (ALL REPEAT.) Or, if no reservation number is given, just ask, "What is *your* name?"

Now for the most important question of all: "Where can I park?" Or "Do you have a parking lot?"

There are many possible answers; so you will have to listen carefully. But if the answer is, "You can use the parking lot next door," then you should ask, "Is it free?" (ALL REPEAT EACH PHRASE.)

It's very common for shops and restaurants to offer *reduced rate* parking at a commercial parking lot.

If so, you might hear, "We'll stamp your ticket." (ALL REPEAT EACH PHRASE.)

Those phrases should cover most situations at any restaurant, theatre, or movie house. So now it's time for the telephone calls.

<u>Notes:</u>   <u>Tasks:</u>

```
┌─────────────────────────────┐
│ PRINT:                      │
│   appropriate response      │
│   ə-prō′-prē-ĭt rĭ-spŏns′   │
└─────────────────────────────┘
```

(Defined pages _____ & _____.)

**DISTRIBUTE COPIES OF ANY NEWSPAPER WEEKEND
ENTERTAINMENT GUIDE,** PREFERABLY ONE TO EACH STUDENT.
YOU WILL NEED AT LEAST TWO IDENTICAL COPIES TO MAKE
PHONE PAIRS. THEN:

GET VOLUNTEER

WHEN DEMONSTRATING, **ANSWER CLEARLY AND FAIRLY.
AVOID GIVING SIMPLE YES OR NO ANSWERS IF YOU CAN
ASK A QUESTION INSTEAD.** MAKE YOUR CALLER BE
SPECIFIC—DRAW THE STUDENT OUT WITH CHOICES TO TEST HIS
COMPREHENSION AND RESPONSES, RATHER THAN MEMORIZED
RESPONSES. **DON'T RUSH. DO HAVE FUN**—THE RESULTS ARE
BETTER. AFTER A COMPLETE "TRANSACTION," THEN:

WAIT UNTIL MOST APPEAR READY. (ABOUT 2 MINUTES MAXIMUM)

WORKING WITH THOSE TWO VOLUNTEERS:

ENTIRE CLASS SHOULD TURN TO THAT PAGE AND AD.

MONITOR THE CONVERSATION. GET COMPLETE THOUGHTS
FROM BOTH PARTIES, USING THE MODELS (BUT NOT NECESSARILY
THE EXACT WORDS) PRESENTED IN OUR "RESERVATIONS" CHART.
ANSWERS CAN BE EITHER FACTUAL OR FANCIFUL, BUT THEY MUST
FULFILL THE INTENT OF THE QUESTION BEING ANSWERED. COACH,
IF NEEDED. WHEN A TRANSACTION IS COMPLETED:

TELEPHONE CALLS EXERCISE

We all look for interesting things to see and do in the newspapers and entertainment magazine. I have brought copies of local entertainment guides so that you can practice asking for information of the kind you might actually need.

Of course we might not know the actual answer to the questions asked, but we can give an appropriate response and continue the conversation.

Before we begin, do you have any questions about the material just completed? (ANSWER FULLY)

I will pretend to be the (restaurant/theatre) with the advertisement on page _____. Please turn to that page. Who is willing to call me for information?

Now, Mr/Ms _____, ask for information you need; and I warn you, I will try to say things you do not expect, because that's normal in telephone calls.

That was interesting. You did very well! So let's have more demonstrations. But first, everyone should choose an advertisement for something you would really like to do. Pick an ad, and look up any new words you will need to use.

Now, who wants to make a call? (GET VOLUNTEER.) And who wants to receive that call? (DITTO.)

The difficult part in making phone calls is that you cannot get or receive visual signals. So I'd like each of you to turn your chair so that you cannot see each other. (WAIT UNTIL IT'S DONE.)

Now, Mr/Ms (caller)_____, what information would you like to get from which ad? Which page?

All right, you may begin. Ring...ring...

<u>Notes:</u>   <u>Tasks:</u>

GET A PAIR TO VOLUNTEER. ASK THEM TO TURN THEIR CHAIRS. **HAVE THE CLASS LOOK UP THE AD BEING USED, AND HEAR AN ENTIRE TRANSACTION.** COMPLIMENT THE PAIR, AND CORRECT ANY ERRORS OR SERIOUS MISPRONUNCIATIONS. THEN PROCEED UNTIL ALL PUPILS HAVE PARTICIPATED IN ONE CALL. THEN REVERSE THE ROLES, SO THAT THE INFORMATION SEEKER IN THE FIRST SERIES BECOMES THE INFORMATION GIVER IN THE SECOND SERIES. IT'S GOOD TO SWITCH PARTNERS SO THE PAIRS DON'T SIMPLY REPEAT THE PREVIOUS, SAFE FORMAT. WHEN FINISHED WITH ALL PAIRED CONVERSATIONS:

That was very good. You see how easy it is to ask for information when you know the common phrases. Let's have another practice phone call.

By now you should have proved to yourself that the telephone is a friend, not a foe. The secret is to be *prepared* for the call you make. Use a pencil and paper to make notes about all the different questions you might have. Write down the answers as they are given to you. Then you will make a *complete* call every time. It's extremely frustrating to call someone and then forget some of the questions. And if you call them back immediately, you can irritate them, too. So do it right the first time—be prepared!

Notes:

Tasks:

NOTE: If only one or two students have these problems, cover this material after class.

NOTE: Tutor, obtain and show copy of local public transit map; lend another, if not given to all.

PRINT: (Transit name)
(Telephone number)

PRINT:
(Major streets)
(Transit transfer points)
(Major routes for bus or train)

CONDUCT GROUP DRILL ON ALL KEY STREET & PLACE NAMES. ALSO PRONOUNCE & DEFINE ALL TECHNICAL TERMS USED COMMONLY BY YOUR SYSTEM, INCLUDING "TIMETABLE" "TRANSFER," "HEADWAY TIME" "FARES" PLUS ANY UNUSUAL USAGES FOUND ON THE PRINTED MAP.

LISTEN AND CRITIQUE/CORRECT. BEGIN WITH VOLUNTEER AND LET EACH PERSON ATTEMPT THE NAMES. IF THEY HAVE TROUBLE, YOU CAN MODEL ALL NAMES FOR THEM TO IMITATE.

OPTIONAL DRILL
PUBLIC TRANSPORTATION

Last session, so many of you indicated problems with the terms and street names of the transit system that I think we should spend a few minutes to review the basics for the benefit of all.

This map is published by our public transit system, called _____. It's free—you can get one with a telephone call. The number is: _____-_____.

Because the overall system is so large, and also because most of us use only a few bus or train lines regularly, we needn't study the entire map. Rather, we will look at the main routes in the central business district. In most cities, that's called the "downtown" area.

The most important street names in the downtown area are these: _____. You can transfer from one line to another at these main transfer points: _____. Now let's practice these names.

Some of us have problems with names of streets and transfer points between our homes and our jobs. Let's practice those, too. I'll lend someone my map. Find your bus or train route on it and pronounce the names of all the transfer points between your home and your job. Who wants to begin?

Before our next class, each of you should phone the transit company and request a copy of the map. Show me your copy when you receive it.

(END OF OPTION)

OPTIONAL DRILL

Notes: Tasks:

MAKE FUTURE ASSIGNMENT:

ANSWER FULLY, IF ANY. COLLECT LOANER DICTIONARIES.

PURPOSE: THE PURPOSES OF THIS SESSION ARE FIRST TO CONSOLIDATE THE GAINS MADE IN THE CONVERSION OF THE WRITTEN WORD WITH ITS DIACRITICAL CODE MARKS INTO STANDARD ENGLISH SOUNDS AND THEN TO BUILD THEIR CONFIDENCE IN USING A STRING OF WELL-PRONOUNCED WORDS IN USEFUL, PRACTICAL PHRASES. IF YOU DO NOT SEE THESE PURPOSES CLEARLY SERVED, RE-READ THE ENTIRE SESSION.

SUMMARY

Even though we weren't perfect this time, I think that you should have proved to yourselves how easy it is to eliminate a foreign accent when you are paying close attention to the correct sounds.

What we have done here today is extremely important in building your command of the English language. We have demonstrated not only that you can reproduce the proper sounds...but also that you can combine those sounds into both words and sentences.

Now you know you can do it! What everybody needs, therefore, is enough practice so that you feel very comfortable with your new knowledge...so that you can use your new dictionary skills confidently.

So next time, please bring a new list of words which give you problems. Here in class, we will check the dictionary codes to find the proper pronunciation for all of them. Your list should have at least a half-dozen words, but not more than ten.

We will begin our class exercises next time with your lists. Then, if time permits, we will make more "telephone" calls using newspaper ads. If you have a particular interest or problem area (food or clothing or cars, for instance), you are welcome to bring your own choice of ad to the class. It's not necessary.

But your list of problem words is essential to the development of your personal vocabulary; so give it the thought it deserves.

That's all for today. Are there any questions?

We'll get together again next _____-day at _____ am/pm. Until then, goodbye/good evening.

END

FOURTH SESSION

F O U R T H   S E S S I O N

Notes: Tasks:

DURING YOUR PRELIMINARY, PRE-CLASS STUDY OF THIS TUTORING
SESSION, LIST MATERIALS NEEDED FOR THE CLASS HERE:

**PREPARE TO REVIEW AND CONSOLIDATE THE BASIC
"CONVERSION TECHNIQUE"** OF TRANSLATING THE
DIACRITICAL MARKS INTO CORRECTLY-PRONOUNCED NEW
VOCABULARY (SLOW/FASTER/NORMAL RATE PRONUNCIATION OF
SYLLABLES). IF YOU DO NOT FEEL SURE OF THIS CONVERSION
TECHNIQUE, REVIEW THE SECOND SESSION NOW. IF YOUR TEXT
DICTIONARY'S PRONUNCIATION KEY USES DIACRITICAL MARKS
THAT ARE SIGNIFICANTLY DIFFERENT FROM OUR COURSE KEY
(TUTOR'S BASIC DRILL CHART), THEN WORK ONLY WITH YOUR
DICTIONARY VERSION FROM THIS POINT ON.

DISTRIBUTE LOANER DICTIONARIES.

**GROUP EXERCISE: MODEL THE KEY WORDS TOGETHER
WITH THE CLASS.** YOU WILL HEAR ANY DISCREPANCIES QUITE
CLEARLY. IF SO, CORRECT AT THE SOURCE BY REPEATING THE
WORDS AS YOU INDICATE THE STUDENT WHO ERRED, REPEAT THE
WORD UNTIL THAT INDIVIDUAL GETS IT RIGHT. WITH THE
POSSIBLE EXCEPTION OF THE "R" SOUNDS, RESPONSE SHOULD BE
CLOSE TO PERFECT. IF NOT, REPEAT THE EXERCISE. THEN GO ON.

**ALLOW TIME FOR STUDENTS TO PRINT PROBLEM WORDS
ON BLACKBOARD.** (IF NONE, USE OVERSIZED CHART PAPER AND
FELT PENS, IF POSSIBLE, AND WORK AT THEIR DESKS.) ALLOW
ABOUT FIVE MINUTES—SOMEWHAT MORE IF SHARING
DICTIONARIES. WHEN MOST ARE FINISHED PRINTING AND
MARKING:

FOURTH SESSION

◄——— DURING ADVANCE PREPARATION, DO THIS

TUTOR: Today we are going to begin with your own list of problem words. After today, they will not be a problem. After we have completed this exercise, we will make more "telephone" calls.

To be sure we don't make mistakes with your problem words, let's review the dictionary key. I think we can all read together.

Please turn to the main Pronunciation Key at the front of the book, page _____. (WHEN READY) Please begin.

You are doing so well with pronunciation that you should not have any problems with your "problem" words. Please print three words from your list on the blackboard. Then print the dictionary's syllabified version with the correct diacritical marks.

I think we can begin. What I would like you to do is to pronounce each of the syllables very carefully, and at a speaking rate much slower than normal. Then, if your sounds are correct, say the word again at a faster rate. Then say it at a normal rate of speech. Are there any questions before we begin? Would you be willing to begin, Mr/Ms _____?

Notes: Tasks:

CHOOSE YOUR BEST STUDENT TO RECITE FIRST, TO SET A HIGH STANDARD. LISTEN CAREFULLY AS THE WORDS ARE FIRST SYLLABIFIED. IF CORRECT, SAY SO AND PERMIT THE STUDENT TO REPEAT AT FASTER AND NORMAL RATES. **IN CASE OF ERROR,** STOP THE STUDENT AT THE END OF THE FIRST SYLLABIFICATION. THEN POINT TO (OR STATE THE NUMBER OF) THE INCORRECT SYLLABLE(S). ALLOW THE SAME STUDENT THE OPPORTUNITY TO PROVIDE THE CORRECT SOUND. FAILING THAT, ASK THE CLASS TO CORRECT THE SOUND. FAILING THAT, YOU PROVIDE THE CORRECT SYLLABLE AND RESTATE THE WORD CORRECTLY.

WHEN EACH WORD HAS BEEN CORRECTLY STATED, REGARDLESS OF THE SOURCE, ASK THE GROUP TO REPEAT IT, SO ALL STUDENTS LEARN ALL "PROBLEM" WORDS. RECITATIONS SHOULD REQUIRE NO MORE THAN TWO MINUTES PER STUDENT.

PERFORMANCE STANDARD: ACCURACY APPROACHING PERFECTION, WITH THE POSSIBLE EXCEPTION OF A TRILLED "R". DO NOT BELABOR THE "R" SOUNDS IF THE ACCOMPANYING VOWEL SOUNDS ARE CORRECT: SOME STUDENTS WILL NEVER LOSE THE TRILL. JUST STRESS THE AMERICAN-R (RETROFLEX-R) IN WORDS YOU MODEL FOR THEIR IMITATION, AND CONTINUE.

ALLOW ABOUT FIVE MINUTES FOR THE CLASS TO WORK AS INDIVIDUALS. WHEN MOST HAVE FINISHED, BEGIN. USE THE SAME TECHNIQUE AS EARLIER: SLOWLY SYLLABIFIED; THEN CONFIRMED/CORRECTED; THEN FASTER AND NORMAL SPEAKING RATES; THEN CLASS REPEATS. CHOOSE A GOOD STUDENT TO BEGIN. MAKE ANY CORRECTIONS BY RE-STATING WORD.

WHEN ALL STUDENTS HAVE READ THROUGH THEIR ENTIRE LISTS, THIS EXERCISE IS COMPLETE. CONTINUE WITH THE PROGRAM.

OPTION: If the preceding exercises have taken less than half the class period, then spend up to ten minutes now to learn new words from the "Vocabulary Drill Chart" (Vowel Sounds/Diphthongs/ Ligatures) from the Third Session, pages 112 to 115.

Many of you probably have a few more problem words on your personal lists. So let's take about five more minutes now to look up each of those words and place the diacritical marks where needed. Work at your own desk and write directly on your list.

Raise your hand if you have a problem.

We will do this exercise just like the blackboard exercise: say the syllables slowly, and if it's correct, repeat it more quickly. Mr/Ms _____, will you begin?)

You are making great progress! I'm very pleased.

IF USING "VOCABULARY DRILL CHART" OPTION: CHOOSE ONE OF THESE TWO METHODS:

1) IF THEIR RECITIATIONS HAVE BEEN NEAR PERFECT, ALLOW THE GROUP TO INITIATE THE PRONUNCIATION OF THE WORDS; OR

2) IF THEY HAVE BEEN UNSURE OF THEMSELVES, MODEL EACH NEW WORD FOR THEM TO IMITATE. YOU CAN SWITCH TO A LISTEN-AND-CORRECT MODE IF THEY PERFORM BETTER THAN EXPECTED.

CONDUCT DRILL AS DESCRIBED ABOVE.

(Optional:)

Let's take just a few minutes to learn more words from the "Vocabulary Drill Chart" that I gave to you last time.

Here is the way we will do this exercise: _____

_____

Mr/Mrs _____, will you begin, please?

<u>Notes:</u>   <u>Tasks:</u>

**PREPARE TO CONDUCT A TEST OF STUDENTS'
UNDERSTANDING OF THE CONCEPTS INVOLVED. SWITCH
GEARS:** PREVIOUS EXERCISES HAVE MEASURED WHETHER THE
STUDENT CAN SUPPLY THE PROPER SOUND FOR A VISUAL CUE—
THE DIACRITICAL MARKS. THIS EXERCISE TESTS THE STUDENT'S
ABILITY TO SUPPLY THE CORRECT DIACRITICAL MARKS TO
REPRESENT THE SOUNDS OF THEIR OWN NAMES. THE LATTER
IS MORE DIFFICULT.

CAUTION: SOME NAMES SOUND DIFFERENT IN THE STUDENT'S
OWN DIALECT THAN IN THE FORMAL OR STANDARD VERSION OF
THE NATIVE LANGUAGE. OBVIOUSLY OUR ENGLISH ATTEMPTS ARE
DIFFERENT FROM EITHER OF THE ABOVE. **THEREFORE, ALLOW
EACH STUDENT TO MARK THE DIACRITICAL AS HE/SHE
ACTUALLY SAYS IT.** SUCCESS OR FAILURE IS MEASURED BY
THEIR ACCURACY IN MARKING THEIR OWN WANTED SPOKEN
SOUNDS.

PRINT YOUR NAME.
MARK THE VOWELS &
STRESS(ES); CONVERT "C" TO "K" OR "S," etc.

STUDENTS PRINT OWN NAMES. EACH PERSON IS EXPECTED TO
INDICATE THE APPROPRIATE DIACRITICAL MARK FOR EACH
VOWEL, PLUS THE STRESS(ES). COACH THEM IF THEY ASK FOR HELP,
BUT *AVOID* PROVIDING THE CORRECT ANSWER. THAT IS, **MODEL
THE SOUND THEY HAVE ALREADY MARKED, BUT DON'T
INDICATE THE NEEDED MARK.** ALLOW 3-5 MINUTES. WHEN
READY:

**MAKE AN HONEST ATTEMPT TO PRONOUNCE ALL
NAMES EXACTLY AS MARKED, EVEN IF YOU KNOW THAT
PRONUNCIATION TO BE INCORRECT.** THIS WILL EMPHASIZE
THE IMPORTANCE OF ATTENTION TO DETAILS, AS MUCH AS TO TEST
THE STUDENTS.

MINI-TEST FOR COMPREHENSION

Now we're going to see whether you really can recognize the small differences in sounds, as indicated by the diacritical marks.

I'd like each of you to go to the blackboard and print your own name. Then mark each vowel with the proper diacritical mark. Place accent marks where needed. If you mark the vowels properly, then every member of this class will be able to say your name exactly as you wish to hear it pronounced.

For example, here's how my name looks. Say it. (CLASS SHOULD PRONOUNCE IT CORRECTLY.)

Now everybody—to the blackboard!

If you have indicated the correct diacritical marks, then I should be able to pronounce your name perfectly on the first attempt.

Notes: Tasks:

IN CASE OF ERROR, THE STUDENT SHOULD POINT OUT THE SYLLABLE(S) THAT DON'T SOUND RIGHT. ASK THE STUDENT TO SUPPLY THE CORRECT SOUND, AND THEN CORRECT THE DIACRITICAL MARK TO AGREE WITH THE WANTED SOUND. IF THERE IS NO GOOD APPROXIMATION OF THE WANTED (FOREIGN) SOUND WITH OUR DIACRITICAL MARKING SYSTEM, SAY SO, AND DO NOT CONSIDER THIS DISCREPANCY AN ERROR.

IF STUDENT FAILS TO SUPPLY THE CORRECT DIACRITICAL MARKINGS, ASK THE CLASS TO SUPPLY IT. FAILING THAT, YOU SUPPLY THE CORRECT MARKINGS.

CONTINUE UNTIL YOU HAVE PRONOUNCED ALL THEIR NAMES ACCEPTABLY. THIS ABILITY TO SELECT CORRECT—OR AT LEAST DEFENSIBLY CLOSE—SOUNDS IS A VALID TEST OF THEIR COMPREHENSION OF THE CONCEPTS.

PERFORMANCE STANDARD: EACH STUDENT SHOULD BE ABLE TO SUPPLY THE CORRECT ADJUSTMENT IF THE FIRST ATTEMPT IS NOT ACCURATE. IF ONE THIRD OR MORE OF ALL STUDENTS FAIL TO PERFORM TO THIS STANDARD, REVIEW ALL THE DIACRITICAL MARKS IN THE "TUTOR'S BASIC DRILL CHART" AND ALSO THE DICTIONARY MAIN PRONUNCIATION KEY.

First is the name of Mr/Ms _____. Did I pronounce it as you expected to hear it?

If *yes:* Good. Class, please repeat: _____.

If not: Then let's find the problem. Please say your name as you expect to hear it. (LISTEN). I am pronouncing according to the markings. Which vowel sound is not familiar to you? (STUDENT SPECIFIES)

What sound do you wish to hear? (STUDENT SPECIFIES)

In that case, the marking should be changed. What is the proper diacritical mark for that sound? Check your dictionary Pronunciation Key...

If I did not pronounce your name perfectly, you are hearing *my* accent in your language. To be perfect, I would need to study your language just as you are now studying English. But you see that the system works well.

You are all becoming quite confident of your new dictionary skills. All the difficult work is now behind you. You have learned to use the dictionary pronunciation key through study of the diacritical codes. That means you are now becoming independent of the classroom when learning new vocabulary. Now you will also begin to lose your accent!

In the last few sessions, we will concentrate on speaking in phrases that reflect the meanings you wish to express.

In order to concentrate on meanings, you should feel more comfortable with the general use of the language. I believe our "telephone" calls help us to depend on our ears more than any other type of classroom exercise. So let's continue with those calls.

Notes: Tasks:

IF SEVERAL STUDENTS HAVE BROUGHT AN AD, YOU CAN PLAN TO PERFORM AS THE PHONE PARTNER BY READING OVER THEIR SHOULDERS WITH THE ONE AVAILABLE COPY.

IF NO ONE HAS BROUGHT IN AN AD, DISTRIBUTE PAIRS OF AD PAGES—OR ENTIRE COPIES OF A LOCAL NEWSPAPER OR MAGAZINE ENTERTAINMENT SECTION. WHEN READY:

```
PRINT: advertisement
  ad-vûr′tĭs-mənt
  ad″vər-tīz′mənt
  ad, ads
```

```
PRINT:
  jargon
  jar'gən
```

```
PRINT:
  bait-and-switch
```

"TELEPHONE" CALLS EXERCISE

Last time, I said we would work on telephone calls to restaurants and theatres. Has anyone brought an advertisement that you find especially interesting?

Everyone has heard the word "ads," meaning *advertisements.* This word has two acceptable pronunciations. The most commonly used form is shown first. Say it. (ALL RESPOND) Now say the other form. (ALL RESPOND)

Advertising is part of the living language. Even though newspapers reach most households, some of the advertisers are addressing only a small part of the total number of newspaper readers.

Therefore fashion advertising uses a different set of words than does entertainment advertising. Expensive restaurants use different words and more foreign words than do the family restaurants, such as McDonald's. An expensive restaurant *requires* reservations, but a family-type or local restaurant might only *recommend* that you reserve in advance.

Any group of special-usage terms, or words, are "jargon."

Although the Federal Trade Commission tries to enforce a doctrine called "Truth in Advertising," not all advertising is honest. Especially when the offer seems to be "too good to be true," it often is! Don't believe it! Ask questions. Ask for brand names and product model numbers, such as for TV sets and air conditioners.

Some retailers use "bait-and-switch" advertising. They advertise a low-priced product and try to persuade you to buy a more expensive one.

Theatres and restaurants cannot do that, of course. However, not all telephone sales people tell you about cover charges, or minimum charges, or parking fees unless you ask. Keep that in mind, as we work today.

Notes: Tasks:

ALLOW 5 MINUTES FOR STUDENTS TO COMPLETE THIS TASK. THEN CONDUCT THE TELEPHONE CALLS IN THE SAME MANNER AS LAST SESSION: PAIRS WORK TOGETHER FACING AWAY FROM EACH OTHER. YOU ARE THE PARTNER FOR ANY AD BROUGHT IN AS A SINGLE COPY. WHEN READY:

IF MULTIPLE COPIES:

OR

IF PAIRED COPIES:

LET ALL STUDENTS HAVE THE OPPORTUNITY TO MAKE OR RECEIVE AT LEAST ONE PHONE CALL. IF TIME PERMITS, REPEAT WITH ROLES REVERSED. AS BEFORE, INVENT INFORMATION, WHEN NONE IS PRINTED, TO KEEP THE GAME GOING.

PERFORMANCE STANDARD: GIVEN TIME PRESSURES, THE STUDENTS MIGHT NOT PERFORM UP TO THEIR INDIVIDUAL CAPABILITIES. EXPECT OCCASIONAL ERRORS. SIMPLY CORRECT THE ERRORS AFTER THE RECITATION, TO AVOID INTERRUPTING THE FLOW OF IDEAS. CHALLENGE ONLY THOSE WORDS WHICH YOU BELIEVE THE STUDENT MIGHT HAVE TRIED TO FAKE: "DID YOU LOOK UP THAT WORD?" ALTHOUGH PRECISION IS DESIRABLE, FLUENCY WITH IDEAS IS MORE IMPORTANT IN THIS EXERCISE.

FUTURE ASSIGNMENT

PRINT: "clipping"

Dictionary page _____.

Take five minutes now to find one advertisement that interests you. Look up the pronunciation, in the dictionary or in your notes, all words that are new to you. Also look up words from your old vocabulary that you are not *sure* you say correctly.

Of course it is a good idea to read the definitions, too, so that you understand the advertiser's intentions (or meanings) before you call. You can mark the ad.

Raise your hand if you have a problem.

Who wants to place the first phone call? (GET VOLUNTEER) Who is willing to answer that phone call? (GET ANOTHER VOLUNTEER)

Who wants to place the first phone call? What page does the ad appear on? (GET PAGE NUMBER) Who else has that same page? (GET RESPONSE) The two of you are now partners for this phone call.

Begin. . .ring, ring.

You are surprisingly capable on the telephone. Is anyone worried about using the phone any longer? (IF SO, ASK WHY: THEN ANSWER OR ASSIST, IF POSSIBLE.)

For next time, I would like you to find a newspaper article about something you understand quite well. It can be about your own country, or a job like yours, or something you are now studying.

Bring a clipping to class. Do you understand the word "clipping"?

(OPTION: If they own dictionaires:)

Be prepared to look up all the new or problem words in the first twenty lines.

You can work on meanings at home from your dictionaries, if you wish.

Notes: Tasks:

COLLECT LOANER DICTIONARIES

PURPOSES: THE PURPOSES OF THIS SESSION ARE FIRST TO
CONSOLIDATE AND REINFORCE THEIR ABILITY TO CONVERT
PRINTED DIACRITICAL CODES INTO CORRECT SOUNDS, AND THEN
TO BUILD THEIR CONFIDENCE IN USING THE NEW SKILLS IN
EVERYDAY CIRCUMSTANCES. IF YOU DO NOT SEE THOSE PURPOSES
CLEARLY, RE-READ THE ENTIRE SESSION.

(In either case:)

Do NOT try to mark pronunciation codes from a different type of dictionary—wait until the next class period to look up words in our dictionary, if you must.

Then we will all read part of our articles to the class. Knowing the meaning of the information will help you to read quickly and accurately.

Using a newspaper article will help to sharpen your conversational skills by making current events an ordinary part of your reading and your vocabulary.

To review: bring one article about a topic you know and are interested in. Look up all the unfamiliar words in the first twenty printed lines, at home or in class. Then we will read some of those lines to the class.

Any questions? (ANSWER FULLY)

We will get together again next _____-day, at ____ am/pm. Until then, goodbye/good evening.

END

FIFTH SESSION

F I F T H   S E S S I O N

Notes: Tasks:

DURING YOUR PRELIMINARY, PRE-CLASS STUDY OF THIS TUTORING
SESSION, LIST MATERIALS NEEDED FOR THE CLASS HERE:

**PREPARE TO REVIEW THE "VOCABULARY (VOWEL
SOUNDS/DIPHTHONG/LIGATURE) DRILL CHART" AND
THE DICTIONARY MAIN KEY** QUICKLY WITH THE ENTIRE
GROUP, PRIOR TO DRILLING INDIVIDUALS. THE GROUP SHOULD
COVER ALL WORDS; INDIVIDUALS, ONE OR TWO WORDS FROM EACH
COLUMN. **DO NOT MODEL ALL WORDS** FOR THE GROUP,
ALTHOUGH YOU CAN MODEL THE INITIAL WORD IN EACH COLUMN
IF THEY HESITATE.

PERFORMANCE STANDARD: EXCEPT FOR "R" SOUNDS, BE
QUITE CRITICAL—BEGIN WORKING TOWARD PERFECTION. DO NOT
PROCEED WITH THE CLIPPINGS EXERCISE UNTIL YOU ARE
SATISFIED WITH OVERALL GROUP AND INDIVIDUAL
PERFORMANCES (OR HAVE ASKED ANY IDENTIFIED LAGGARDS TO
REMAIN AFTER CLASS).

DRILL GROUP AS INDICATED ABOVE.

DRILL INDIVIDUALS; ONE OR MORE WORDS IN ROTATION, AS
NEEDED.

**DISTRIBUTE LOANER DICTIONARIES. DRILL THE GROUP
QUICKLY, USING THE DICTIONARY MAIN KEY.** IF
SATISFACTORY, GO ON TO THE CLIPPINGS. IF HALF OR MORE HAVE
MISSED ONE OR MORE WORDS, DRILL AS INDIVIDUALS. SEPARATE
THE CAPABLE FROM THE MARGINAL PERFORMERS. MARGINALS
MUST REMAIN AFTER CLASS TODAY AND IN FUTURE DAYS TO AVOID
HOLDING BACK THE CAPABLE PEERS.

FIFTH SESSION

◄——— *DURING ADVANCE PREPARATION, DO THIS*

TUTOR: Before we begin working with the clippings you were asked to bring today, let's be sure that the sounds of the English language are very clear in our ears. Quickly, as a group, read down each column of the "Vowel Sounds" from the Vocabulary Drill Chart.

Now I want to hear each of you make each of those sounds...perfectly, if possible. Read one word in each column, each person reading the next word in the column. Ready? We'll begin with Mr/Ms _____.

Some of the sounds are absolutely perfect. I feel very pleased, and I congratulate you. Let's spend just a few more minutes with the dictionary main key, at the front of the book.

Soon you will have a rich new vocabulary, and then English conversation will be fun.

Notes: Tasks:

POINT OUT "EARS"
ON ANY PAGE

PAGE _____.

EXCEPTION: NO "EARS" FOUND ON LETTER-CHANGE PAGE IF FULL PAGE.

USING DICTIONARY PAGE "EARS"

How many remembered to bring a clipping about your own country or job or field of study? We will look up the new words of the article in just a few minutes.

Before we begin, let me give you a tip to help speed your search for words: Use the "ears" at the top outer corners of each page.

Notice that two words appear on each ear. The first word printed there is also the first word defined on that page. The second word printed in the ear is the last word defined on that page.

If the spelling of the word you are seeking falls between those two ear words, then your word appears on that same page. Otherwise, keep searching.

When doing dictionary reference work, use only the ears. Do not waste your time looking in the middle of the pages—there are too many pages in the dictionary.

As a quick exercise, look up the word "ear" in the dictionary. Use the ears. Who has found it? (WORK WITH VOLUNTEER) Which of the definitions seems most appropriate for our usage? (NO. _____—DISCUSS?)

In journalism, the term "ears" refers to the information sometimes printed in the top corners of the front page. Because that's a special usage, the journalism definition is not given in this abridged dictionary. However, you would find that usage given in most college editions and all unabridged dictionaries.

Now, if I say, "This course will sharpen your ears," which sense of the word am I using? (NO. _____)

When doing your homework, be sure you read all the usages listed, so you interpret the meanings correctly.

And who has noticed the exception to the ears rule? (DISCUSS)

As you should have learned by now, the only rule that applies to this course is "There are no firm rules." Keep aware, always.

Notes: Tasks:

SINCE ABOUT HALF OF ALL STUDENTS USUALLY FORGET TO BRING
A CLIPPING, **BE PREPARED TO PROVIDE EXPENDABLE
NEWSPAPERS AND/OR MAGAZINES** SO THE WORK CAN
BE DONE NOW. ALLOW ABOUT TEN MINUTES FOR PREPARATION.
ADD DIACRITICAL MARKS ON THE CLIPPINGS—A USEFUL HABIT
FOR THEM.

WHEN MOST ARE FINISHED:

LISTEN! JOT DOWN THE MAJOR COMPLAINTS, IF ANY, AND
DISCUSS ALL BEFORE PROCEEDING:

_____
_____
_____
_____
_____

NOTE: The most common complaint is usually time-pressure; just reassure them that it gets easier with practice. Other common complaints include multiple entries, discrepancies with diacritical markings, or difficulties with a specific word. Discussion material follows: use it only if needed.

FOR PROBLEMS REGARDING:

NEWSPAPER ARTICLES EXERCISE

Now let's go on with our assignment.

Look up all words that are new to you, or words in your old vocabulary that you are not sure of. Be sure you check alternate entries to find the *meaning* that's appropriate. About twenty lines will be enough. Raise your hand if you have a problem.

Did you find that easy? (PROBABLY NOT) What was the most troublesome aspect for you?

1) *Multiple entries:*
     Some words appear two or more times because they have two or more totally different meanings. Because they sound the same, we call such words *homonyms,* meaning "same-name."
     Some words function as different parts of speech: as a noun or verb or adjective, for instance. Each of these uses could affect the pronunciation, as well as the meaning. Always be sure to check the part of speech that's appropriate for the meaning intended.

     You are developing real mastery of our textbook dictionary. I'm proud of you. But real life can present problems: you might not always find this brand when you need a dictionary. So you must be able to function with any dictionary available.
     (END OF MULTIPLE ENTRIES DISCUSSION)

Notes: Tasks:

```
┌─────────────────────────┐
│ PRINT:                  │
│   plane = plān          │
│   rain = rān            │
│      -also              │
│   plane = pl ⃞a  n       │
│   rain = r ⃞a  n         │
└─────────────────────────┘
```

NOTE: Some unabridged dictionaries allow
for regional variations in pronunciation. So
the words "cot" and "caught" might be
shown as the same or different vowel sounds.

**IF SO, THAT STUDENT SHOULD PRINT THE PROBLEM
WORD ON THE BLACKBOARD. CHECK THE DIACRITICAL
MARKINGS IN THE DICTIONARY BEFORE ALLOWING THE
STUDENT TO PRONOUNCE IT.** DO NOT ALLOW ANY WORD TO
BE MISPRONOUNCED. IF THE STUDENT IS UNSURE, ALWAYS ASK FOR
THE SPELLING (OR LET THEM PRINT).

BE ALERT TO THE POSSIBILITY THAT A STRESS MARK COULD
TOUCH A BAR, ARC, OR TENT AND APPEAR TO CREATE AN
UNFAMILIAR, UNTRACEABLE "NEW" MARK.

2) *For discrepancies with diacritical markings:*
     As we have already discussed in earlier lessons, each dictionary publisher uses different codes or key words to indicate sounds. However, the basic sounds of English are the same no matter how they are coded.
     Also, the system of comparing the markings of the needed word with the markings of the dictionary's pronunciation key remains the same.
     For example:

     If you learn to say the key words correctly as listed in the dictionary pronunciation key, that marking always means that sound—everywhere in the dictionary. I could use a square or a triangle as a marking...but the *system of comparing* remains the same, always.
     If you already own an American-English dictionary that's different from our class text, bring yours to class next time. I will review the key words with you to be sure there are no problems.

(END OF DIACRITICAL MARKINGS DISCUSSION)

3) *For problems with pronunciation of specific words:*
     You should not have a problem with any word if you have accurately indicated the diacritical markings.
     Because the dictionary print is so small, sometimes it's a little bit difficult to distinguish between two types of marks. If so, then the problem lies in misreading the print, not in your ability to pronounce.
     Did anyone have a problem because you are not able to determine which marking is used?

(END OF PRONUNCIATION DISCUSSION)

Notes: Tasks:

PRINT:
 phrase
 predicate adjective
 adverbial clause
 prepositional phrase

PRINT:
 sentence

PRINT:
 paragraph

PRINT: "Punctuation"
 periods
 capitals
 commas, etc.
 conjunctions
 parentheses

PHRASING FOR SENSE

One of the problems with attempting to read in a new language is that we concentrate too much on the individual words...and not enough on the meanings or the sense of the phrases and sentences created by those words. That's normal.

But even though it is normal for the speaker, it is often difficult for the listener to understand.

All conversation is best understood when the sense of the communication is clear *while it is being spoken.* Yes, we can ask for a word to be repeated, but that takes our attention away from the communication and toward one word among many. The result: misunderstanding, delay, and frustration.

You can help to convey the sense of your words by grouping them into "phrases." A phrase is a group of several words which are related by the thought or meaning they express. Some examples are predicate adjectives, which modify nouns; adverbial clauses, which modify verbs; and prepositional phrases, which we'll discuss in a few minutes.

All the words used together to express one complete thought are called a "sentence."

Several sentences used together to express a complex thought or special relationship are generally united into a single "paragraph."

In all Western languages written with an alphabet, visual clues to phrases are used called "punctuation."

These include (a) periods to end a thought; (b) a capital letter to start a new thought/sentence; (c) and comas, semicolons, colons, elipses (dots), and dashes—all these help us to indicate units of a series or conjunctions; and (d) parentheses, used to indicate helpful (but not necessary) information. Sometimes that parenthetical information is marked with commas. You studied punctuation during grammar lessons. Now let it help you communicate *sense*.

Notes: Tasks:

```
┌─────────────────────────┐
│ PRINT:                  │
│  phrasing               │
│  frāz-ing (iŋ)          │
│  punctuation            │
│  pŭŋk″chŏŏ-a′shən        │
│  function words         │
│  fŭŋg′shən              │
└─────────────────────────┘
```

```
┌─────────────────────────┐
│ PRINT:                  │
│  A tall, thin, shiny    │
│  metal pole.            │
└─────────────────────────┘
```

```
┌─────────────────────────────┐
│ PRINT:                      │
│  "The real problem, according│
│  to the President, is money."│
└─────────────────────────────┘
```

RE-READ THE SAME SENTENCE ABOVE, GIVING IT STRESSES THAT AFFECT THE IMPLIED MEANING.

RE-READ STRESSING "REAL."

RE-READ STRESSING "MONEY."

```
┌─────────────────────────┐
│ PRINT:                  │
│  context                │
│  kŏn′tĕkst″             │
└─────────────────────────┘
```

Definition page ____.

When reading aloud—or speaking on the telephone—it is especially important to use logical phrasing. English has two key indicators of phrases: punctuation and function words.

Punctuation, such as periods and commas, alerts us visually to relationships among ideas when we are reading. But when we are speaking, we must give those same clues with our voices.

In reading aloud, I could say all those words without pausing: (RUN WORDS TOGETHER) "A tall thin shiny metal pole."
Or I could help you to understand by saying: "A tall, thin, shiny metal pole." Now let's take another example:

A neutral reading says "The real problem, according to the President, is money."
In a newspaper article, it is necessary to tell us who is speaking. Therefore the phrase "according to the President," is set off by comas. That could be the entire purpose of the reporter.
But if we emphasize that same phrase "according to the President," we suggest several possible things: First, that although the President thinks so, many others might not agree. Or second, we can imply that the idea is debatable, or unusual, or even foolish.

It is also possible to change the meaning slightly by stressing other words. For instance, if we stress the word "real," we suggest that the other problems previously mentioned are secondary.

If we emphasize "money," we suggest that we have located a basic culprit above all others.

Then which of all these interpretations is correct?
Only the writer knows for sure. However, we should be able to understand the writer's intentions from the context of the material.

Notes: Tasks:

PRINT: "Conjunctions"
and, but, for, nor,
or, so, yet

PRINT: "Connectives"
only, still, then, also,
thus, hence, if...then,
therefore, nevertheless,
not only...but also

NOTE: Some students might not understand
these terms of grammar. It is not possible to
cover English grammar in this brief course.
Therefore the scripted explanations must
suffice for class. Recommend that needy
students enroll in an appropriate level of
grammar course.

PRINT:
intonation
list intonation

Because the intended sense of the material must guide the spoken emphasis, you must study all material you prepare for class. You must understand the material before you can make the class understand it when reading aloud... or when making telephone calls.

So punctuation, reflected in the voice, helps us to convey meaning.

The function words also help us convey meanings. Function words are markers that tell us relationships among ideas. They *do* things rather than *mean* things.

Among function words are the conjunctions:

Repeat these words, please: "And, but, for, nor, or, so, and yet."

Other connectives—or conjunctive adverbs—also help us to understand relationships among ideas. Here are some of the commonly used connectives:

Read these words aloud. I'll listen. (ALL READ)

When conversing or reading aloud, we also use the voice in ways that are known as intonations. If I say "no," it matters whether I am stating a fact or expressing anger or correcting a child. We say the word differently each time, although it is the same word.

Notes: Tasks:

PRINT:
soup, salad, roast beef,
baked potato, sweet peas,
chocolate cake, coffee

(YOUR VOICE SHOULD RISE AT THE LAST SYLLABLE OF EACH
INTERIM FOOD ITEM AND FALL ON THE LAST SYLLABLE OF THE
LAST WORD.)

PRINT:
preposition
prepositional phrase
object of the preposition

Also we use the voice to indicate a continuation of an idea—or a list of ideas—or to ask a question.

For instance, the voice always rises when we are asking a question. For instance, "Can you hear me?"

The voice also rises at the end of each segment of a series. At dinner we ordered:

We ordered soup...salad...roast beef...baked potato...sweet peas... chocolate cake...and coffee.

If I read this list correctly, you knew the list was not complete until the word "coffee."

At the end of a sentence...or at the end of a list...the voice always falls to indicate the end.

In conversations, we listen for these indicators so that we do not needlessly interrupt the speaker. If you develop a habit of helping your listener with intonations, conversations will flow more smoothly.

One of the most common—and therefore most important—of the function word categories is that of the preposition.

The preposition itself, plus all the words that stand between the preposition and the first noun that follows, is called "a prepositional phrase". In grammar, the noun following the preposition is known as the "object of the preposition."

If you learn to recognize and be guided by prepositions, you will become very skilled at interpreting and phrasing ideas. Phrases express units of meaning.

Notes: Tasks:

PRINT:
  prepositions:

PRINT:
  to, from, in, over,
  under, for (etc.)

NOTE: Some pupils might not understand these grammatical terms. Suggest that they enroll in needed English classes. You cannot teach grammar now. Don't try. For our purposes, just describe the "object of the preposition" as the first noun that follows the preposition.

USING PREPOSITIONAL PHRASES

We use these words hundreds of times every day without even thinking about them. The list includes: to, from, in, over, under, for, and many, many more. We'll review them in a few minutes.

As you learned in your grammar classes, both the preposition itself *plus* its object *plus* all the object's modifiers belong in the prepositional phrase. The object of the preposition is always a noun or a pronoun. For example, we can say "to the man" or "to him." Usually they relate to people or places in everyday conversation. Say, "preposition." (ALL REPEAT.)

For example, we can say "to the store" or "to the grocery store" or "to the new grocery store." We are certain that all those words relate to each other because they are all part of the prepositional phrase.

So we indicate that relationship in conversation, or when reading aloud from a book, by speaking those words *as a unit.*

For instance, you might ask why I didn't answer my telephone when you called.

I can say, "I went to the *store.*" That brief answer suggests that the type of store doesn't matter—I was away from my telephone.

Or I can say, "I went to the *grocery* store and then to the *shoe* store." That suggests that I'm too busy to sit and wait for your phone call.

But if I say, "I went to the *newest* grocery store," then you know that curiosity was just as important as the groceries. Or you might know that the new grocery store is farther away and therefore took more time.

Notes: Tasks:

PRINT:
(Phrase as spoken)

**DEMONSTRATE PHRASING:
CHOOSE AN ARTICLE NOT PICKED BY ANY STUDENT.
THEN READ THE FIRST COUPLE OF SENTENCES ALOUD.
FIRST, EXAGGERATE THE PAUSES INDICATED BY THE
COMMAS, AND GROUP THE PREPOSITIONAL PHRASES
CAREFULLY. NEXT, REPEAT THE SAME MATERIAL AT
NORMAL SPEAKING SPEED AND WITH NORMAL, MORE
SUBTLE, PAUSES.**

PRINT ON BLACKBOARD OR DISTRIBUTE COPIES OF KEY
PREPOSITIONS CHART, ON THE FOLLOWING PAGE. **MODEL
SENTENCES FOR SEVERAL COMMON PHRASES;**
WITH THE CLASS REPEATING.

**INDIVIDUAL DRILL IS NOT NECESSARY UNLESS YOU
DETECT A NUMBER OF ERRORS.** CORRECT ANY ERRORS
IMMEDIATELY. CONCENTRATE ON IDEAS, NOT DETAILS. A VERBATIM
EXAMPLE FOLLOWS. CONDUCT THE BALANCE OF THE DRILL ON
THAT PATTERN.

Prepositional phrases can be very useful in understanding the other person, too, because the speaker is telling you which thoughts belong together.

Sometimes we use one prepositional phrase to modify the object of another. For instance: "The book is *on* the chair *against* the far wall."

Where is the book? Is it against the wall? Or does the second prepositional phrase tell you where the chair is? (GET ANSWER: CORRECT ANY MISUNDERSTANDINGS)

So the meaning of this sentence is: The book is *on* a chair; and the specific chair, among several, is in that specific location. Yet it's the chair, not the book, that's located against the wall.

Now let's practice using the commas and prepositional phrases to express units of thought.

Isn't that easier to understand than a string of words with no clues offered? (THEY SHOULD AGREE.) Here's a list of the prepositions we use every day.

PRACTICAL WORD POWER

Key Prepositions and Phrases Chart

aboard (aboard the train)
about (about the book/about seven
   o'clock/all about us)*
above (above your head)
across (across the street)
after (after breakfast/after all)
against (against the law/against the wall)
along (along the river bank)
amid (amid the flowers)
among (among several people)
around (around the corner/seen around)
at (at the movies/at 7pm/at last/at once)
before (before class ends/stand before
   the flag)
behind (behind the desk/behind the times)
below (below the average)
beneath (beneath the surface)
beside (beside the door)
besides (besides us)
between (between us)
beyond (beyond what is expected/beyond
   the river)
by (by the dozen/by the window/by car
   or train)
concerning (concerning your grades)
despite (despite the weather)
down (down the stairs)
during (during the program)
for (for that reason/for the first time)
from (from my cousin/from Mexico/
   from now on

in (in the water/in the afternoon/in haste)
inside (inside the box)
into (into the car)
like (like the other one/I like ice cream)
near (near my home)
of (of many things/of mine)
off (off the airplane)
on (on the table)
onto (onto the wagon)
outside (outside the fence)
over (roll over/over the target/over there)
regarding (regarding that discussion)
since (since my last visit)
through (through the doorway/through
   their help)
throughout (throughout the night)
till (till the clock strikes midnight)
to (to me/to that end)
toward (toward the sun/toward that end)
under (under the canopy)
until (until further notice)
up (up the stairs)
upon (upon seeing her/upon the table)
with (with everything else)
within (within the closet/within ten minutes)
without (without wasting more time)
via (via air express/to Washington via
   New York)

* Prepositions with two or more senses are
  are shown:
  Preposition (example of first sense/second
  sense/third, if any).

Double Prepositional Constructions

in addition to (the other items)
in back of (the store)
in case of (emergency)
in front of (that wall)
in place of (the lost book)
in spite of (all our efforts)
instead of (walking, take a cab)
on top of (the desk/everything else...)

Idiomatic Expressions

out of (out of gas/out of my way/out of
   danger)
up to (up to $5/if left up to us)
due to (due to the rain/money due to her)
up above (the sky up above)
up on (sitting up on the roof)
all about (tell all about it/scattered
   all about)

SUGGESTED DRILLS: Each student should construct a complete sentence using one of the given examples; then create a different sentence for the same preposition. Repeat until each student has modeled at least three sentence pairs correctly.

KEY PREPOSITIONS EXERCISE

To begin, let's pronounce each of the key prepositions in our list.
(ALL REPEAT ALL PREPOSITIONS)

Now let's concentrate on the meanings and the uses of these phrases. In a prepositional phrase, we group together all the words that are part of a single idea.

Say "Aboard the train...or plane...or ship." (ALL REPEAT.) Say "We talked about the book." (ALL REPEAT) Say "I usually eat dinner...about seven o'clock." (ALL REPEAT.) Say, "We were sitting...on the grass...with the books/spread... all about us." (ALL REPEAT.)

Notice that there are three common meanings for the preposition "about." With practice, you will use all the meanings of all the prepositions correctly. But you should be aware that whatever the meaning, the phrase consists of the preposition itself plus all the words between the preposition and the first noun.

Additional phrases can provide new information, as in the last practice sentence. Read the phrase as a unit.

Say, "...on the grass...with the books/spread...all about us." (ALL REPEAT.)

(NOTE: Distribute copies of "Key Prepositions and Phrases" chart.)

Now it's your turn to make phrases. Use this list. Each person can take the next word in the list. Give us a *complete sentence* using the preposition. You may borrow the samples here or provide your own, as you wish.

Mr/Ms _____, would you begin?

Notes: Tasks:

UPON COMPLETION OF THE DRILL USING PROPOSITIONAL
PHRASES CHART, CONTINUE:

```
┌─────────────────────────────────┐
│ PRINT:                           │
│   We went (from the store)       │
│   (to the movies.)               │
│                                  │
└─────────────────────────────────┘
```

HELP STUDENTS TO PREPARE, IF HELP IS REQUESTED. WHEN
THEY ARE FINISHED MARKING PREPOSITIONAL PHRASES, THEIR
CLIPPINGS WILL HOLD THE MARKINGS OF BOTH PRONUNCIATION
AND PHRASING. NOW THEY ARE READY TO RECITE. BEGIN:

**LET A VOLUNTEER BEGIN, IF POSSIBLE. LISTEN
CAREFULLY. DO NOT INTERRUPT** ANY STUDENT'S RECITATION
UNLESS THE EXERCISE IS POORLY PREPARED. JUST JOT DOWN
NOTES AND CORRECT ON COMPLETION OF THE TWENTY LINES.
MISPRONUNCIATIONS SHOULD BE RARE, AND PHRASINGS SHOULD
BE FAIRLY ACCURATE. CONCENTRATE ON IDEAS.

**IF ANY STUDENT HAS TRIED TO FAKE THE PRONUNCIATION
OF ANY WORD,** HE/SHE MUST PRINT IT ON THE BLACKBOARD
AND MARK THE DIACRITICAL CODES, USING THE DICTIONARY.
VERIFY THE MARKINGS. IF INCORRECT, ASK FOR A CORRECTION. IF
CORRECT, ASK THE STUDENT TO PRONOUNCE SLOWLY, BY
SYLLABLE, THEN FASTER, THEN AT NORMAL SPEAKING RATE.
WHEN CORRECTLY SPOKEN, THE CLASS CAN REPEAT.

COMPLIMENT THE BEST FEATURE OF EACH READING.

**UPON COMPLETION OF THE READING EXERCISES,
SUMMARIZE:**

CLIPPINGS EXERCISE

No, I have not forgotten that we plan to read from the newspaper clippings. However, good reading skills require *both* correct pronunciation *and* phrasing for sense, or meaning.

Therefore, we will now spend five minutes to allow you to mark all the prepositional phrases you find in the first twenty lines of your clipping. For example:

Use parentheses to indicate each phrase unit. Mark the phrases directly on the clippings. Do that now. Raise your hand if you have a problem.

Most of us have finished marking; so we can start. Each person will read to the class the first twenty lines. Pronounce the words carefully, and let us hear the prepositional phrases. This is not a speed-reading exercise. Take your time. Be comfortable with the material...so we can understand its meaning.

Who is willing to begin?

Notes: Tasks:

ALLOW TEN MINUTES TO PREPARE. THEN CONDUCT THE RECITATIONS IN THE SAME PATTERNS AS IMMEDIATELY PRECEDING. WHEN ALL STUDENTS HAVE FINISHED READING AND HAVE HEARD YOUR CORRECTIONS AND CRITIQUES:

USING THE STUDENT'S CLIPPING, READ ALOUD THE SAME TEN LINES JUST RECITED. SPEAK CLEARLY AND SLIGHTLY MORE SLOWLY THAN NORMAL SPEAKING RATE. EMPHASIZE MEANING. ASK EACH STUDENT TO REPEAT EACH MEANINGFUL PHRASE AFTER YOU UNTIL ALL TEN LINES HAVE BEEN COVERED. THEN ASK THE STUDENT TO READ ALONE, ALL TEN OF THE SAME LINES, FROM HIS OWN CLIPPING.

PERFORMANCE STANDARD: PRONUNCIATION SHOULD BE NEARING PERFECTION. PHRASING SHOULD BE CORRECT, ALTHOUGH THE STUDENT MIGHT BE SOMEWHAT HESITANT ABOUT GROUPING THOUGHTS EXPRESSED BY GERUNDS OR OTHER MARKERS OF PHRASING-FOR-MEANING. **DO NOT BELABOR ERRORS RELATED TO GRAMMAR**—JUST CORRECT THEM. INDICATE THAT GRAMMAR CONTROLS AND THAT THE STUDENT DID NOT MAKE AN ERROR ON CLASSROOM LEARNING.

COLLECT LOANER DICTIONARIES

You have done quite well as a class. It seems that the mistakes made in pronunciation were the result of trying to fake it—to guess at pronunciation because you were already familiar with the written word.

Old vocabulary is often a problem because you have learned it with your native vowel structure. It will change only if you listen and try to change.

New vocabulary that you're learning in this class is practically perfect. As your vocabulary grows, all of your conversations will be increasingly free of your troublesome accent.

The combination of correct pronunciation and phrasing according to meaning will put you in command of the English language, both in speaking and in listening. Conversations with Americans who speak standard American-English will now start to be fun.

The skills you have just learned—to mark pronunciation and phrasing directly on the material—is so important that we should do one more exercise.

Take ten minutes now to prepare ten more lines from the same article. Place diacritical marks and phrasing units on the clipping. Work to the end of the nearest complete paragraph—perhaps nine or eleven lines. Begin.

Now let's put more of the rhythm of the language into the readings. I'll read those same ten lines back to you, and then you repeat them after me. May I have your clipping, Mr/Ms _____?

Those of you who have already studied English grammar might be interested in learning other indicators of phrasing for meaning. A very good source for the review of prepositional phrases and other phrase markers is contained in the book entitled *Dictionary of Prepositions for Students of English,* by Eugene J. Hall. (New York, Minerva Books, Ltd., 1982.)

Notes: Tasks:

FUTURE ASSIGNMENT:

OPTIONS:

1) **IF YOU ARE CONDUCTING THE BASIC EIGHT SESSION COURSE CONTAINED IN THIS WORKBOOK,** THEN THIS CLASS PERIOD IS ENDED. JUST SIGN OFF:

2) **IF YOU ARE AN EMPLOYER OR SOCIAL SERVICES VOLUNTEER AND WISH TO INSERT *ONE* SPECIAL LESSON** COVERING VOCATIONAL OR JOB-SPECIFIC VOCABULARY, HERE ARE POSSIBLE ALTERNATIVES:
   a) NINE SESSIONS: 1, 2, 3, 4, 5, FULL-SESSION INSERT, 6, 7, 8.
   b) NINE SESSIONS: 1, 2, 3, 4, 5, HALF-SESSION INSERT/HALF OF 6; HALF-SESSION INSERT/SECOND HALF OF 6; 7, 8.

3) **EXTENDED NINE-PLUS SESSIONS:** ONLY 1, 2, 3, 4, 5, 6, 7, 8 plus INSERT, INSERT, INSERT (as needed).

IMPORTANT: UNDER NO CIRCUMSTANCES SHOULD THE COURSE AS STRUCTURED IN THIS WORKBOOK BE INTERRUPTED BY MORE THAN ONE FULL-SESSION INSERT. TO DO SO WILL BREAK THE CONTINUITY OF INSTRUCTION. THAT WILL RISK MORE THAN CAN BE GAINED BY AN EARLY INTRODUCTION OF JOB-SPECIFIC VOCABULARY AND PHRASES.

INSTRUCTIONS FOR OPTIONS 2-a and 2-b FOLLOW. SUGGESTIONS FOR OPTION 3 CAN BE FOUND THERE, AS WELL.

IF PRESENTING ANY INSERT(S), CHOOSE A METHOD NOW AND PREPARE THE NECESSARY MATERIALS FOR HANDOUT IN CLASS.

ANNOUNCE THE ADDITIONAL COURSE MATERIALS:

SUMMARY

We have now covered all the basic information relating to pronunciation and phrasing. In all the remaining sessions, we will work on making your speech pattern smooth and natural. That will help you to express your thoughts very effectively. . .every time.

Remember, the purpose of conversation is to create understanding between two or more individuals. Everything that contributes to the ease of understanding also contributes to language skills and also to your enjoyment of working with others.

For next time select another article. Again, it should be about a topic you are interested in. Place your diacritical marks and phrasing marks on the first twenty lines. Please complete that work before you come to class. Use your "Vocabulary Drill Chart" and your list of prepositions to guide you.

As we discussed earlier today, some dictionaries use slightly different codes. If you already own any other type of dictionary, bring it to class next time. Do not use it for this assignment until I have reviewed it with you.

Notes: ## Tasks:

THE PURPOSE OF THIS SESSION IS TO MOVE THE STUDENT FROM
THE PRONUNCIATION OF ISOLATED WORDS TOWARD A PHRASING
CONDUCIVE TO THE SENSE OF THE SPOKEN MESSAGE. THIS SKILL
REQUIRES A FAIR AMOUNT OF COACHING; SO DO NOT DEMAND
PERFECTION OF PHRASING TODAY. DO EXPECT NEAR-PERFECTION
OF ALL PRONUNCIATION, WITH THE POSSIBLE EXCEPTION OF THE
"R" SOUNDS. IF YOU DO NOT SEE THAT PURPOSE CLEARLY IN THE
EXERCISES PROVIDED, RE-READ THE ENTIRE SESSION.

(OPTIONS PAGES FOLLOW)

Standard phrases are also important tools of communication on-the-job. To help make daily life easier in the workplace, we will practice some of the most common phrases next time

(Additional comments, if appropriate:) _____

_____

_____

Until next session, goodbye/good night.

END

Model for optional

VOCATIONAL INSERT
(Initial Sequence)

IF YOU ARE INSERTING A SPECIAL, JOB-RELATED SEQUENCE, PROCEED AS FOLLOWS:
 1) PREPARE A HANDOUT SHEET OF SPECIAL TERMS AND COMMON PHRASES: USE THE KEY PREPOSITIONS CHART AS YOUR GUIDE.

 2) AS A WARM-UP, REVIEW THE KEY PREPOSITIONAL PHRASES FROM THE FIFTH SESSION. MODEL THE CORRECT PHRASING IN REPEAT-AFTER-ME STYLE, AND MOVE QUICKLY.

 3) DISTRIBUTE YOUR SPECIAL, JOB-RELATED HANDOUT(S). MODEL EACH WORD AND PHRASE, WITH THE CLASS REPEATING AS A GROUP. WHEN THE GROUP IS PRONOUNCING ALL WORDS AND PHRASES ACCURATELY, ASK INDIVIDUALS TO READ ALONE. CORRECT EACH PERSON AS NECESSARY, SO THE MATERIAL IS SPOKEN PERFECTLY (OR AS CLEARLY AS THE JOB REQUIRES, IF MATERIAL IS HIGHLY TECHNICAL). NOTE:* UNLESS YOU HAVE ENOUGH MATERIAL TO FILL THE ENTIRE CLASS PERIOD, DO NOT USE MORE THAN HALF THE PERIOD FOR THIS JOB MATERIAL. INSTEAD, REVIEW NEXT TIME.

 4) IF USING ONLY HALF THE PERIOD, USE THE REMAINING 45-60 MINUTES TO RETURN TO THE STANDARD COURSE: BEGIN THE SIXTH SESSION EXACTLY AS WRITTEN. COMPLETE IT UP TO THE POINT WHERE DENOTATIONS AND CONNOTATIONS ARE INTRODUCED, PAGE 205. THEN STOP. NOTE:** BE PREPARED TO BEGIN AT THIS SAME POINT AT THE NEXT SESSION. USE ANY REMAINING TIME FOR DRILLS.

 5) (OPTIONAL) IF A REVIEW OF JOB-RELATED MATERIAL IS NEEDED NEXT TIME, ALLOW ABOUT 10-20 MINUTES FOR A QUICK, REPEAT-AFTER-ME DRILL AT THE NEXT SESSION, AND ANNOUNCE THAT REVISED LESSON PLAN NOW. APPROPRIATE WHETHER SIXTH SESSION IS STARTED OR NOT.

 6) MAKE AN ASSIGNMENT FOR THE SIXTH SESSION. EACH PUPIL SHOULD PREPARE ABOUT TWENTY LINES MORE FROM THE FIFTH SESSION ARTICLE. USE A NEW ARTICLE IF THE SIXTH SESSION IS DELAYED. MENTION THAT THEY SHOULD ATTEMPT TO PHRASE ACCORDING TO THE WRITER'S INTENTIONS; THAT IS, THE APPARENT MEANINGS. MARK PREPOSITIONAL PHRASES.

 7) COMPLIMENT THE GROUP FOR THEIR PROGRESS, AND SAY GOODBYE.

If you choose to review the job-related materials next time, review the Vocational Insert Follow-up Sequence, following.

*IMPORTANT: If the vocational or job-specific materials will require more than one full session, do not interrupt the original standard course of eight sessions. Instead, tag the whole of the job-related materials at the end of the course, and give the material as much time at the end of the course, and give the material as much time as you feel it deserves.

**IMPORTANT: Decide now whether to commit an entire (extra) session to the job material. Choose one full period or two halves. Up to fifteen minutes of job-related words and phrases can be squeezed into the existing lesson plans. If more time is needed, you must allow for a ninth session, whether as an insert between Five and Six or has a combination with first- and second-half of Six on two days.

Model for optional

VOCATIONAL INSERT
(Follow-up Sequence)

IF YOU USED AN ENTIRE (EXTRA) CLASS PERIOD FOR THE VOCATIONAL SEQUENCE, YOU MAY NOW CHOOSE TO:
  1) BEGIN THE ORIGINAL SIXTH SESSION NOW AND COMPLETE IT AS WRITTEN, WITHOUT INTERRUPTION, IN THE SEVENTH TIME SLOT; OR

  2) CONDUCT A QUICK REVIEW OF THE JOB-RELATED/VOCATIONAL MATERIAL BEFORE BEGINNING THE SIXTH SESSION, EXACTLY AS WRITTEN.

IF YOU STARTED THE SIXTH SESSION AND INTERRUPTED IT, AS RECOMMENDED, AT THE POINT OF DISCUSSION OF DENOTATIONS AND CONNOTATIONS, PAGE ___. YOU MAY NOW CHOOSE TO:
  1) CONDUCT A QUICK REVIEW OF THE JOB-RELATED MATERIAL BEFORE BEGINNING AT THE BREAK POINT, OR

  2) PICK UP THE DISCUSSION AT THE BREAK POINT AND COMPLETE THE SIXTH SESSION WITHOUT INTERRUPTION.

ACT ON YOUR CHOICE:

- BEGIN THE SIXTH SESSION FROM THE START (IGNORE THIS PAGE), OR

- START YOUR REVIEW SESSION BY MODELING THE CORRECT PRONUNCIATION FOR THE MOST IMPORTANT TERMS AND PHRASES FROM THE SPECIAL HANDOUT. THE CLASS SHOULD REPEAT, EACH TIME. LISTEN FOR PRONUNCIATION AND PHRASING OF THE GROUP, AND CORRECT THE INDIVIDUAL WHO MAKES ANY ERRORS. (DO NOT EXCEED 15-20 MINUTES) AND:

- THEN RE-ENTER THE SIXTH SESSION SCRIPT AT THE BREAK POINT BY SUMMARIZING:
  Last time we were learning how to give interpretations relating to the sense of the information being discussed. We learned that by reading the entire article before preparing small sections, we can determine how the writer wishes to have his words interpreted. Today we are going to continue with that concept.
  NOW GO TO THE BREAK POINT AT THE DENOTATION/CONNOTATION SECTION, PAGE ___, AND COMPLETE THE SESSION AS WRITTEN.

END OF VOCATIONAL INSERT
SPECIAL INSTRUCTIONS

EMPLOYER OPTION

EMPLOYER OPTION

SIXTH SESSION

SIXTH SESSION

Notes: Tasks:

DURING YOUR PRELIMINARY, PRE-CLASS STUDY OF THIS TUTORING SESSION, LIST THE MATERIALS NEEDED FOR THE CLASS HERE:

PREPARE TO CHANGE THE EMPHASIS OF THE CLASSROOM FROM GENERAL INFORMATION WHICH ALL STUDENTS MUST MASTER TO SPECIFIC ASSISTANCE NEEDED BY THE INDIVIDUAL STUDENT.

PERFORMANCE LEVEL: EXPECT VIRTUAL PERFECTION IN THE PRONUNCIATION OF FAMILIAR MATERIAL, SUCH AS THE "BASIC TUTOR CHART," "VOWEL SOUNDS/DIPHTHONG/LIGATURE DRILL CHART," AND THE MAIN AND PAGE-BOTTOM DICTIONARY PRONUNCIATION KEYS. THEY COULD BE HESITANT IN FORMING NEW MULTI-SYLLLABIC WORDS, BUT ENCOURAGE THEIR USE OF THE SLOW/FASTER/NORMAL RATE CONVERSION TECHNIQUE. THE TRILLED "R" SOUNDS ARE ACCEPTABLE WHEN THE WORD IS CLEAR.
IF ANY INDIVIDUAL HAS FAILED TO MASTER THE FAMILIAR MATERIAL, A PROBLEM EXISTS. KEEP THE STUDENT AFTER CLASS AND DRILL TO PERFECTION OR REFER TO A SPEECH PROFESSIONAL. DO NOT HOLD BACK THE CLASS.

DISTRIBUTE LOANER DICTIONARIES. LISTEN AND CRITIQUE/CORRECT. PROCEED AS OUTLINED ABOVE. IF YOU HEAR NO SIGNIFICANT ERRORS, GO ON TO NEXT TOPIC. IF MINOR ERRORS, CORRECT THEM IMMEDIATELY BY REPETITION. WHEN SATISFIED, CONTINUE THE DRILL. WHEN READY TO GO ON TO NEXT TOPIC:

SIXTH SESSION

◄———— *DURING ADVANCE PREPARATION, DO THIS*
Note: to accommodate the optional vocational insert, this lesson material can be used in the Seventh or Sixth/Seventh split time slots)

TUTOR: By this time, I expect you to pronounce the Dictionary Key words perfectly. So without my help, please read as a group from the dictionary's main and page-bottom keys.

Some of you own different types of dictionaries, and these will have slightly different symbols. Did you remember to bring those dictionaries?

IF NONE OWNED: Then we have no problem.

IF FORGOTTEN: Be sure to bring it in next time. Please do not use it for pronunciation until we have reviewed it together.

IF YES: The sounds will be the same, of course, even though the diacritical marks might be slightly different. Let's pronounce the key words together.

Notes: Tasks:

MODEL ALL THE KEY WORDS FOR ALL VOWEL SOUNDS IN
EACH DIFFERENT DICTIONARY. BY READING OVER THE SHOULDER
OF THE OWNER, YOU CAN BOTH HEAR AND COACH, IF NECESSARY.
THE GROUP SHOULD REPEAT THESE KEY WORDS. WHEN YOU HAVE
DEALT WITH ALL DICTIONARY BRANDS:

CHECK FOR PREPARATION. USUALLY ONE OR MORE HAVE
FAILED TO PREPARE ADEQUATELY. ALLOW THEM TO WORK ALONE
WHILE THE REST OF THE GROUP CONTINUES. **PROVIDE A
NEWSPAPER FOR STUDENT USE,** SINCE THEY RARELY
REMEMBER THE NEWSPAPER IF THEY HAVE FORGOTTEN TO DO THE
ASSIGNMENT. IF HALF OR MORE OF THE CLASS HAVE FAILED TO
COMPLETE THE MATERIAL, ALLOW FIFTEEN MINUTES TO MARK
DIACRITICAL CODES AND PHRASES.

**TO AVOID PENALIZING STUDENTS ALREADY PREPARED,
GIVE SPECIAL ATTENTION** BY REVIEWING THE MARKED
ARTICLES AND ANSWERING QUESTIONS, ETC.

WHEN READY TO BEGIN:

CONDUCT INDIVIDUAL READING EXERCISES. VOLUNTEER
SHOULD READ THROUGH THE ENTIRE TWENTY-LINE SELECTION.
DO NOT INTERRUPT—JUST JOT DOWN ANY ERRORS AND
CORRECT ON COMPLETION OF THE READING. **COMPLIMENT
THE STUDENT BEFORE CORRECTING.** AFTER THE FIRST
READING ONLY, EXPLAIN:

As I said before, you can use any American-English dictionary after
I have reviewed the key words with you. Please do not use the British-English
dictionaries for pronunciation, because many sounds, stresses, and even spelling
are quite different.

NEWSPAPER EXERCISE

Now, let's go on to new things.

Your assignment for today was to choose a new article about your native
country or your job or a topic about which you have some knowledge. You
should already have marked the diacritical codes and prepositional phrases.
Is everyone prepared?

As we discussed last time, phrasing according to the sense of the message is
the most helpful communication technique you can offer your listener, apart
from correct pronunciation.

When you read aloud to the class today, read at a comfortable speed. Pay
close attention to your sounds and to your units of meaning—your phrasing.
Who is willing to begin? (GET VOLUNTEER)

That was a very good first reading. You seem to understand the idea of
phrasing. What you need now is practice...plenty of practice. With practice you
will develop fluency and confidence. You can sound just like this:

Notes: Tasks:

**BORROW THAT STUDENT'S CLIPPING AND READ
SEVERAL LINES TO MODEL** THE CORRECT PHRASING OF THE
PASSAGE, UNINTERRUPTED BUT CAREFULLY PHRASED. **THEN GO
BACK AND RE-READ** THE SAME FEW SENTENCES, THIS TIME
PAUSING SLIGHTLY TO INDICATE PHRASING FOR SENSE. **RE-READ
A THIRD TIME,** ASKING STUDENTS TO REPEAT EACH SEPARATE
PHRASE, AS INDICATED PREVIOUSLY. **FINALLY, ASK THE
"OWNER" OF THE ARTICLE TO RE-READ** AT A NORMAL
RATE FROM THE SAME LINES.

IF THE CLASS IS SMALL, ALL STUDENTS CAN RE-READ ALL
TWENTY LINES. TIME LIMITATIONS GOVERN; ALLOW FIVE TO TEN
MINUTES PER STUDENT, CALCULATED SO THAT ALL STUDENTS
COMPLETE THIS EXERCISE WITHIN THE FIRST FULL HOUR OF THE
PROGRAM (OR SECOND HOUR, IF A HALF-SESSION INSERT OF
VOCATIONAL PHRASES IS USED).

AFTER ALL STUDENTS HAVE FINISHED:

GET THEIR COMMENTS AND DISCUSS.

Do you think we have made the precisely-correct interpretation of each clipping each time? That is, do you think the writer of the articles will say we are accurately conveying his intended meaning?

When I made today's assignment, I asked you to choose an article about something you know or are interested in. The reason is that we must be familiar with the general subject matter and also with the content of the entire article before we are relatively sure of interpreting it correctly.

The next time you prepare a few lines for reading aloud in class, be sure you read the entire article before marking the few lines assigned.

<u>Notes:</u>   <u>Tasks:</u>

OPTIONS:
1) IF A VOCATIONAL HALF-SESSION INSERT WAS MADE, THEN THIS CLASS PERIOD IS COMPLETED. IF SO, SIGN OFF:

COLLECT LOANER DICTIONARIES

2) IF NO VOCATIONAL INSERT WAS MADE, OR IF A FULL-SESSION INSERT WAS MADE, THEN NO BREAK IS NECESSARY HERE. THEREFORE, GO DIRECTLY FROM THE PRECEDING PAGE TO THE FOLLOWING TASK AND SCRIPT PAGES 204 AND 205, IGNORING THE "ALTERNATE END" PROVIDED ABOVE.

OPTIONAL BREAK POINT

(re: Vocational Insert)

For next time, prepare twenty more lines from the same article. We want to be sure that you are taking advantage of the understanding already developed.

Mark your pronunciation and phrasing as before, and be prepared to make the class really *understand* what the writer is trying to tell us: all forty lines!

Until next session, goodbye/good night.

(ALTERNATE END POINT)

OPTIONAL BREAK POINT

<u>Notes:</u>   <u>Tasks:</u>

IF THE SIXTH SESSION WAS INTERRUPTED LAST TIME
BECAUSE OF A VOCATIONAL HALF-SESSION INSERT, THEN PLACE
THE SECOND-HALF SESSION MATERIAL HERE. DITTO IF ONE FULL-
SESSION VOCATIONAL INSERT TOOK OVER THE SIXTH SESSION TIME
SLOT—OKAY TO SPEND TEN MINUTES REVIEWING VOCATIONAL
MATERIAL HERE—BUT NO LONGER!

WHEN READY TO CONTINUE THE WORKBOOK COURSE:

```
WRITE:
factual, fair
unbiased, impartial
```

```
PRINT:
denotation
dē″nō-tā ′shən
connotation
kŏn″ə-tā ′shən
```

DENOTATIONS AND CONNOTATIONS

There are two important facts to consider when attempting to interpret written material. First, no matter how carefully we study the article, we can never be absolutely certain that we know what the newspaper reporter, or writer, intends with every line. The better the writer, the more certain we can be.

Second, although it would be wonderful if every writer were absolutely factual and fair...also called unbiased or impartial...writers are human, and their own emotions sometimes creep into the writing.

Say "factual...fair...unbiased...impartial." (ALL REPEAT)
Very few, if any, writers are absolutely free of bias toward their topic. Instead of choosing neutral words, many writers use words that have what we call "judgmental elements." Such elements can prejudice our response to the article, favorably or unfavorably.

That means that although any word conveys a particular *denotation,* it also conveys a *connotation.*

The "denotation" names the thing or the category of meanings. The "connotation" indicates an attitude or feeling or judgment toward that thing in this particular usage of that category of meanings.

For instance, you will often hear the words "expensive...inexpensive...and cheap." All three words pertain to cost. That is, they *denote* money amounts. Therefore, there is some element of factual or objective description, within the money category.

However, there is a great deal of difference in the *connotations* of these same three words.

Notes: Tasks:

PRINT: expensive

PRINT: inexpensive

PRINT: bargain

PRINT: cheap

PRINT: overpriced

PRINT: quality

PRINT: value

PRINT:
Roget's Thesaurus
Rō′zhā′s thĭ-sôr′əs

When we say that something is *expensive,* we mean that its cost is high in dollars relative to its own kind of goods. That is, an expensive car and an expensive hat are different amounts by many thousands of dollars. Yet we understand the meaning to be "More than the average cost."

When we say that something is *in*expensive, we mean that its dollar cost is low or a very good value—less than the usual price for such a thing. That is generally a compliment. We also often use the word "bargain," to indicate that we have saved money wisely.

However, if we say that a thing is "cheap", we sometimes mean that it costs fewer dollars than a quality item should. That often implies that the "cheap" thing is poorly made or otherwise undesirable. When you hear the word "cheap," it is wise to ask the speaker whether he or she is recommending or criticizing, since *price vs. quality* should be at issue.

Finally, we sometimes say that an item is "overpriced." By that we mean that we can buy the same item or similar quality elsewhere for less money.

As you can see, the *de*notation of all these words is cost or money-related. The *con*notation is *value*-related, and value reflects subjective judgment.

Connotations of words are extremely important to any language. In most unabridged dictionaries, only the denotations are given. If you will be using the word in an important document, look it up in an unabridged dictionary—or ask a native-speaker for help.

If you have frequent need to understand the exact connotations of new words, then you should become familiar with *Roget's Thesaurus.*

Say "Roget's Thesaurus." (ALL REPEAT.)
The thesaurus is a wonderful reference book. It will tell you the connotation of the word you have in mind. But under the category of the denotations, it will list many other words, each with its connotation. The thesaurus can actually help you find a better word, if there is one.

Notes: Tasks:

HELP STUDENTS PREPARE. ALLOW ABOUT FIVE MINUTES MAXIMUM. WHEN **MOST ARE READY, BEGIN A DISCUSSION.** ALLOW FIVE MINUTES OVERALL.

NO COURSE CAN OFFER "ANSWERS" FOR ALL THE WORDS THAT MIGHT BE FOUND TO COLOR OR BIAS THE BASIC INFORMATION OFFERED IN ANY ARTICLE. **USE YOUR COMMON SENSE:** IF AN ARTICLE SAYS A POLITICIAN'S SPEECH WAS "BRILLIANT," YOU HAVE A PRIME EXAMPLE. NEUTRAL WORDS WOULD POSSIBLY INCLUDE "DOCUMENTED" OR "TEN MINUTE" SPEECH. "GOOD," "BAD," OR "LONG-WINDED" ARE CLEARLY SUBJECTIVE. FOCUS ON POSSIBLE BIAS, NOT POLITICAL CONTENT.

DISCUSS ONE OR TWO WORDS FROM EACH STUDENT'S CLIPPING. IF THEY HAVE CHOSEN SUBJECTIVE OR JUDMENTAL WORDS, YOU KNOW THEY UNDERSTAND THE CONCEPT. THEN GO ON TO THE NEXT TOPIC.

IF ABOUT HALF OF THE STUDENTS INDICATE WORDS THAT DO NOT EXPRESS ATTITUDE OR JUDGMENT, THEN EXPLAIN WHY THE WORDS OFFERED ARE NOT VALID EXAMPLES. CHOOSE BETTER EXAMPLES FROM THEIR CLIPPINGS. THIS IS COMPLEX LANGUAGE STUDY—DO NOT EXPECT PERFECTION. WHEN READY:

Now let's try to put this new information to work.

Look through your clipping and circle those words that you think reflect the writer's subjective attitude or judgment toward the material. It can be favorable or unfavorable. . .it can also be obvious or very subtle.

Take just a few minutes now to find and circle any words that you think are not neutral. Begin with the lines prepared for today. We will try to determine whether our interpretation should be changed.

That was somewhat difficult, wasn't it?

Don't be concerned. Sensitivity to any new language develops only slowly. When you have that sensitivity, you have mastered the language.

The important lesson for us is that the writers express judgments with the particular words they choose. We must identify the connotations of the words before we can decide whether to believe the writer's version of the events.

Why do you suppose I am putting so much emphasis on interpreting the newspaper?

Notes: Tasks:

LEAD A DISCUSSION. TWO BASIC REASONS:
1) NEWSPAPERS PROVIDE MOST INFORMATION ABOUT THE WORLD
TO MOST PEOPLE WHO WANT MORE DETAILS THAN THE TV
NEWSCASTS PROVIDE.
2) NEWSPAPERS REFLECT THE LIVING LANGUAGE; WHEREAS BOOKS
ARE OFTEN VERY FORMAL AND SO DO NOT TEACH CURRENT USAGE
AS WELL.

DO NOT STATE THESE REASONS. RATHER, LEAD THE
STUDENTS TOWARD THESE CONCLUSIONS BY ASKING RELATED
QUESTIONS. ALLOW FIVE MINUTES OVERALL.

TWO PURPOSES: FIRST, TO UNDERSTAND COURSE CONTENT;
SECOND, TO BEGIN DISCUSSING COMPLEX IDEAS WITHOUT THEIR
BEING AWARE THAT IT IS HAPPENING. AFTER THE FACT, MAKE A
POINT OF IT:

THEY SHOULD AGREE. **DISCUSS BRIEFLY** IF THEY HAVE
INTEREST AND QUESTIONS.

**BEGINNING WITH VOLUNTEER, EACH STUDENT SHOULD
READ THE TWENTY LINES PREPARED FOR TODAY.**
CRITIQUE AS DISCUSSED IN OPENING NOTES FOR THIS SESSION.
USE ALL REMAINING TIME LESS TEN MINUTES NEEDED FOR
"HEADLINES" TOPIC.

Are you aware that we have been discussing some very complex ideas relating to the English language?

It is clear to me that you have better English conversation skills than you realize. Part of the problem is that you might be somewhat self-conscious.

Probably everyone was nervous when reading from their clippings...but no one was nervous while we were discussing these ideas about newspapers and the judgments they lead us toward. Correct?

Now I think we're ready to read and interpret the clippings correctly. Who is willing to begin?

READ SEVERAL HEADLINES FROM YOUR NEWSPAPER.

SELECT AND READ ALOUD ANOTHER HEADLINE.

SELECT ANOTHER HEADLINE, BEGINNING WITH A VERB THAT SEEMS TO COMMAND RATHER THAN REPORT. DISCUSS ITS LIKELY FULL GRAMMATICAL FORM. WHEN THEY COMPREHEND, CONTINUE:

SHOW THE EDITORIAL PAGE OF YOUR LOCAL NEWSPAPER. CALL ATTENTION TO THE UNSIGNED OPINION IN THE EDITORIAL COLUMN, AS WELL AS TO THE SIGNED-OPINION COLUMNS, OFTEN WITH WRITER'S PHOTO.

FUTURE ASSIGNMENT

UNDERSTANDING HEADLINES

Many people have problems with the newspaper headlines—those large-print titles at the top of each article.

Part of the problem arises because space is very scarce; therefore, the sentence meaning and descriptions must be condensed into the fewest possible words.

The other part of the problem is that to achieve the condensed form, the newspaper editor often eliminates important "function" words, such as pronouns and auxiliary verbs. Usually the infinitive form of a verb is used instead of the exact tense. These changes can be confusing.

Therefore we might find a headline that reads: "President to Go to Paris" instead of "The President will go to Paris," or even "The President is planning to go to Paris."

The important point is that newspaper headlines do not reflect the correct grammar you have learned—so you should not feel responsible for the confusion. But you *can* learn to interpret the headlines.

We also see headlines that begin with a verb, as in "Find Buried Treasure." Of course we understand that somebody *has found* a buried treasure. Yet the statement used in the headline is an imperative mode. If a headline reads..."Find Buried Treasure"...it tells *me*, if it is strictly interpreted, that I should go out and *find a treasure.*

All newspapers have an editorial page. There the editors and managers tell you what *they* think about the news. Bias is expected and permitted in editorials and signed opinion columns.

What should we learn from all of this?

Obviously, we must bring good sense and some good amount of thoughtful effort to our newspapers. Then we can truly understand how little fact and how much opinion or conjecture is being conveyed in any "news" article.

When we can separate fact from fiction, we are on the road to becoming well-informed citizens.

For next time, I would you to spend another half hour to prepare in advance of class. Use the same article as you have already used today. Please make notes now regarding your assignment:

First, interpret the headline on your article. Write it out as a complete sentence, including function words. That might require only one or two words to be added. Do not write an explanation—just provide the missing words. You can write them directly on the clipping.

Notes: Tasks:

VERIFY THAT ALL STUDENTS HAVE UNDERSTOOD ALL THE POINTS OF THE ASSIGNMENT. IF NECESSARY, REPEAT.

IMPORTANT: IF STUDENTS DO NOT OWN THEIR DICTIONARIES, THIS WORK MUST BE DONE IN CLASS NEXT TIME. ADJUST THE ASSIGNMENT COMMENTS ACCORDINGLY.

COLLECT LOANER DICTIONARIES

THE PURPOSES OF THIS SESSION ARE FIRST TO CONFIRM AND EXPAND THEIR ABILITY TO PHRASE COMPLETE THOUGHTS AND THEN TO BEGIN SENSITIZING THEM TO THE SUBTLETIES OF THE LANGUAGE.

IF STUDIED IN GREATER DETAIL, THIS IS PROBABLY SENIOR-HIGH OR COLLEGE-LEVEL MATERIAL; SO BE PATIENT AND HIGHLY ENCOURAGING. IF YOU DO NOT SEE THESE PURPOSES CLEARLY, RE-READ THIS ENTIRE SESSION.

Second, read very carefully through the entire article twice—or more, if necessary—until you believe you understand what the writer intends with his choice of words. Review all the lines prepared for class today and decide whether you have interpreted them correctly. If not, supply the correct interpretation next time.

(IF STUDENTS OWN DICTIONARIES:)

Third, prepare about twenty *additional* lines for reading aloud next time. Look up the pronunciation *and the meanings* of all new words; and mark the prepositional phrases.

(IF NOT:)

Third, prepare about twenty *additional* lines for reading aloud next time. If possible, look up the meanings of new words. We will look up the diacriticals in class; mark the prepositional phrases.

Next time, you will read all forty lines to the class and then tell us whether you agree or disagree with the writer. Is the article fair or biased? Be prepared to tell us your reasons.

This is an important assignment. If you do this exercise well, you will prove to yourself and to your classmates that you are beginning to develop a feeling for the English language. That is the point at which your mastery of the language begins.

So spend some time with your clipping. And come to class prepared to surprise me!

Any questions? (ANSWER FULLY.)

That's all for today. See you next _____-day at _____ am/pm.

END

SEVENTH SESSION

S E V E N T H   S E S S I O N

Notes: Tasks:

DURING YOUR PRELIMINARY, PRE-CLASS STUDY OF THIS TUTORING
SESSION, LIST THE MATERIALS NEEDED FOR THE CLASS HERE:

ALL EMPHASIS IN TODAY'S CLASS IS DIRECTED TOWARD THE
INDIVIDUAL NEEDS OF THE VARIOUS STUDENTS. YOU WILL BE
LISTENING AND COACHING, BUT THERE IS NO "LECTURE" TO
BE DELIVERED. ANY DISCUSSIONS WILL RESULT FROM THEIR
COMMENTS AND PROBLEMS. YOU ARE NOT EXPECTED TO BE AN
AUTHORITY ON THE WORLD—YOUR OWN CONTRIBUTION RELATES
TO USAGE OF YOUR OWN LANGUAGE. YOU HAVE A LIFETIME OF
EXPERIENCE. USE IT. IF YOU DON'T KNOW A SPECIFIC ANSWER,
SAY SO AND OFFER TO LOOK IT UP.

***IF STUDENTS DON'T OWN DICTIONARIES, DO THE
WORK NOW. IF ABOUT HALF THE CLASS HAS FAILED TO
PREPARE,** ALLOW ABOUT 15 MINUTES FOR THE CLASS TO WORK
ON THE ASSIGNMENT. THOSE WHO HAVE ALREADY PREPARED
SHOULD **CONVERSE WITH EACH OTHER AND YOU ON
ANY ITEM OF INTEREST—CORRECT ANY SERIOUS
MISPRONUNCIATIONS.** WHEN READY TO PROCEED:

**GIVE THE FIRST VOLUNTEER SOME AMOUNT OF
LATITUDE IN THE PRESENTATION:** DO NOT EXPECT OR
REQUIRE ANY PARTICULAR AMOUNT OF TIME FOR ANY SEGMENT
OF THE PRESENTATION IF HIS/HER COMMENTS SHOW A
COMPREHENSION OF THE IDEAS. **CORRECT, IF NECESSARY,
AND COMPLIMENT. THEN CONTINUE** WITH EACH OTHER
STUDENT IN TURN. ANY ADJUSTMENTS YOU WISH TO MAKE IN
PROCEDURE CAN BEGIN WITH THE SECOND STUDENT'S RECITATION.
AVERAGE TIME WILL BE ABOUT 5 MINUTES PER STUDENT,
MINIMUM; LONGER IF YOU ENCOURAGE DISCUSSION OF THE
MATERIALS READ ALOUD.

WHEN READY TO PROCEED:

SEVENTH SESSION

◄——— *DURING ADVANCE PREPARATION, DO THIS*

TUTOR: Your assignment for today was a continuation from last time. First, you should have re-interpreted the headline in correct grammatical form. Then re-read the article to examine the writer's intent. And then be prepared to read aloud an additional twenty lines. Has everyone completed that assignment?*

Here's what I'd like you to do during your presentation to the class:

First: read the headline as written; then tell us a proper grammatical form.

Second: tell us whether your writer used few or many subjective terms; then, whether you agree or disagree with his interpretation of the events reported, and *why.*

Third: Read the forty lines of copy which you have prepared, paying close attention to both pronunciation and phrasing.

To summarize, that's headlines; agreement or disagreement; and reading aloud. Who wants to begin?

Notes: Tasks:

BE PREPARED TO PROVIDE NEW NEWSPAPER CLIPPINGS. DISTRIBUTE NOW.

AT THE END OF TEN MINUTES, **DETERMINE WHETHER MOST ARE READY.** IF NOT, EXTEND THE TIME FOR ANOTHER FIVE MINUTES. THEN BEGIN:

HEAR AND CRITIQUE RECITATIONS. DURING THE PRESENTATION, LISTEN FOR ALL THESE ELEMENTS:
1) **HEADLINES**—DOES THE STUDENT UNDERSTAND THE HEADLINE MESSAGE?
2) **INTERPRETATION**—DOES THE STUDENT COMPREHEND THE GIST OF THE SUBTEXT AS CONVEYED BY THE CONNOTATIONS OF THE SUBJECTIVE WORDS?
3) **PRONUNCIATION**—IS THE STUDENT "CONVERTING" THE DIACRITICAL CODES CORRECTLY FOR ALL THE LINES PREPARED FOR TODAY?

IF TIME PERMITS, DISCUSS SUBTEXTS AND HIDDEN MESSAGES IN THE DELIVERED MATERIAL. MOST POLITICAL ARTICLES ARE RIPE! MAKE NOTES SO YOU CAN DISCUSS THE MOST OBVIOUS AND MOST SUBTLE EXAMPLES. (BALANCE OF PROGRAM TAKES ONLY THREE MINUTES.)

FUTURE ASSIGNMENT:

Today you have demonstrated that you understand not only the words, but also the messages of these articles. And that indicates that you are beginning to master the language, not only its pronunciation.

What you have done here today is extremely important. Because of its importance, I think we should do one more short exercise on a new article.

Here's what we'll do. First, pick an article from these newspapers. Then give us the correct grammatical form of the headline. Tell whether you agree or disagree with the writer and why. Then read the first ten lines to the class. Take ten minutes now to do that. I'll answer any questions individually.

Some of you are not finished, but because our exercise is based on critical reading of ideas we can begin. If you have not looked up the new words in all ten lines, it's okay to read only as far as you have finished.

Do I have a volunteer to begin?

It's obvious that you are aware of the emotional overtones conveyed in the newspaper articles. As you become even more familiar with the language, you will find yourself making critical judgments about most of the articles you read. And that's smart!

Next time will be our final session.

I'd like you to prepare an original three minute presentation to the class regarding your own native country. You can tell us about a national holiday or about a very unusual custom—or anything of interest.

Plan your presentation in advance, because I want you to be sure to look up the pronunciation of every new word...and every difficult old word in your vocabulary.

Notes: Tasks:

COLLECT LOANER DICTIONARIES

PURPOSE: THE PURPOSES OF THIS SESSION ARE TO CONSOLIDATE
THE PREVIOUS LEARNING OF DIACRITICAL CODES AND PHRASING
FOR SENSE, OR MEANING; THEN TO DEMONSTRATE THAT ABILITY
IN PRACTICAL USAGE. IF YOU DO NOT SEE THOSE PURPOSES
CLEARLY, RE-READ THIS ENTIRE SESSION.

What you talk about is much less important than that you make a clear presentation of the ideas, using the proper pronunciation and suitable phrasing.

If several of your countrymen are in this class, it might be a good idea to choose different topics.

We will begin the class next time with your oral presentations. Then we will end the course with the final exam I promised during the first session. Do you remember what it is? (ANSWER:) Each of you will open the dictionary to three different pages and take the longest word on those pages—and pronounce it!

That's the entire exam. And I know you can pass it!

We'll have an interesting class next time. See you then.

END

EIGHTH SESSION

EIGHTH SESSION

DURING YOUR PRELIMINARY, PRE-CLASS STUDY OF THIS TUTORING SESSION, LIST THE MATERIALS NEEDED FOR THE CLASS HERE:

IN THIS FINAL SESSION **YOU WILL BE FUNCTIONING AS A COACH AND CRITIC.** BY NOW, YOU KNOW QUITE ACCURATELY THE SPECIFIC TYPE(S) OF PROBLEM(S) EACH INDIVIDUAL MIGHT BE HAVING. LISTEN FOR THOSE TROUBLE SPOTS AS EACH RECITES. COMPLIMENT. THEN PROVIDE A FEW WORDS OF GUIDANCE FOR FUTURE EFFORT BY EACH INDIVIDUAL IN TURN. THEN ENCOURAGE OTHER MEMBERS OF THE CLASS TO ASK QUESTIONS. THE NATURE OF THE DICUSSION EACH TIME IS MUCH LESS IMPORTANT THAN THE FLUENCY OF THE CONVERSATION. CORRECT ANY SERIOUS MISPRONUNCIATIONS, OF COURSE; BUT LET THE IDEAS FLOW!

PERFORMANCE STANDARD: NEAR PERFECT PRONUNCIATION, GOOD PHRASING, AND MUCH-IMPROVED FLUENCY (EACH STUDENT VS. SELF)

CONDUCT ORIGINAL PRESENTATION EXERCISE. LET YOUR VOLUNTEER BEGIN, AND CRITIQUE **THE RECITATIONS AS JUST STATED ABOVE.** ALLOW AT LEAST 5 MINUTES PER PRESENTATION, OR ONE FULL HOUR SHARED, WHICHEVER IS MORE. THEN:

E I G H T H   S E S S I O N

◄———— *DURING ADVANCE PREPARATION, DO THIS*

TUTOR: Welcome to our final session. I find it hard to believe that our course is nearly complete—the time went so fast. But I'm also aware that each of you has worked quite hard and made tremendous gains in pronunciation and new vocabulary. That means you are much nearer your goal of mastery of the English language than you were only a few weeks ago.

Today's assigned presentations are designed to let you see how well you can express yourself in English when you are confident of both your topic and your pronunciation. And we build confidence with practice.

I'll ask each of you in turn to make his three-minute presentation. Then I'll take just a moment to make suggestions or corrections, if needed; and then the class will have a few minutes to ask questions about your presentation and your country. In this mixed group, you are considered an expert in matters of your country and your selected topic—so relax. Speak slowly and distinctly...and tell us your story.

Who is willing to begin today?

You have all made great advances in your English language skill, and I'm proud of you. Now it is time for the wonderful event you have been waiting for—the final examination!

As we learned early in this course, all publishers of dictionaries use their own set of key words and diacritical codes. But the system of comparing the Pronunciation Key to the needed word does not change.

Regardless of what type of dictionary you are using, the basic sounds of American-English remain the same.

<u>Notes:</u>

<u>Tasks:</u>

DISTRIBUTE LOANER DICTIONARIES

LEAD A QUICK READING OF THE TEXT MAIN KEY, FOLLOWED BY THE PAGE-BOTTOM BRIEF KEY. DO NOT READ WITH THEM: LISTEN FOR ERRORS. THERE SHOULD BE NO ERRORS IN FAMILIAR WORK, BUT IF ANY, CORRECT IMMEDIATELY BY REPETITION OF THE MISPRONOUNCED WORD(S). THE TRILLED-R CAN BE IGNORED IF THE WORD IS CLEAR, BUT MODEL THE AMERICAN-R (RETROFLEX-R) FOR GOOD MEASURE. WHEN THE DRILL IS COMPLETED:

CONDUCT THE TEST, BEGINNING WITH YOUR BEST STUDENT. HIS/HER PERFORMANCE WILL PROVE THE COURSE THESIS AND SET A STANDARD FOR OTHERS. HEAR THREE WORDS FORM EACH STUDENT TESTED. **PERFECTION IS POSSIBLE,** AND ACCEPTABILITY OF PRONUNCIATION IS VIRTUALLY CERTAIN.

VIEW ALL STUDENT RECITATIONS IN PERSFECTIVE! BECAUSE THESE STUDENTS WILL BE BETTER SERVED BY PERSONAL CONFIDENCE THAN BY ONE FINAL CORRECTION, **PROVIDE CORRECTIONS OF ONLY SERIOUS ERRORS.** OTHERWISE, YOUR INTERIM MODELING WILL SERVE THE SAME PURPOSE VERY SUBTLY. COMPLIMENT THEM!

WHEN ALL HAVE COMPLETED ALL THREE WORDS:

COLLECT LOANER DICTIONARIES

To simplify today's exam, we will work only with the diacritical codes and sounds found in our text. To be sure our ears are holding only the correct sounds, let's read the dictionary's main key together:

Now we are ready to begin. When I call on you—not before—open your dictionary at random. Then tell the class which pages you are using. The classmates will observe.

Then choose the longest word you see. Spell it. Then pronounce each syllable very carefully, including the stresses. If you are correct, I will say so, and you should then repeat the pronunciation at a normal rate of speaking. I will repeat to verify, and then the class will repeat. So everyone here will learn to pronounce all the test words correctly.

Mr/Ms _____, please open your dictionary to a random page and find the longest word there.

We're finished! Congratulations.

If you will think back over the entire course, you will remember that the most serious errors were always made by those who attempted to guess. That's just faking it...and we can always spot a fake.

So do yourself a favor; use the skills you have developed: use the dictionary. Take the minute or two required to look up a new word. Then you'll say it correctly for the rest of your life.

Then the marvelous and rich English language will serve you...also for the rest of your life.

Thank you for working so hard...because that has made my time with you worthwhile.

Good luck...and goodbye.

END

PURPOSE: THE PURPOSE OF THIS SESSION IS TO BUILD EACH
STUDENT'S CONFIDENCE IN HIS OWN ACHIEVEMENT BY
DEMONSTRATING HIS COMPETENCE IN BOTH SOUND CONVERSION
AND "PUBLIC" SPEAKING. ALL YOUR EFFORTS SHOULD BOLSTER
THEIR CONFIDENCE.

IF YOUR STUDENTS CAN PERFORM THEIR FINAL EXAM PERFECTLY (OR
NEARLY SO), THEN YOU HAVE SUCCEEDED AS A TUTOR/TRAINER.
CONGRATULATIONS! AFTER ONE OR TWO MORE REPETITIONS OF
THE COURSE, YOU WILL FIND YOURSELF RESPONDING TO THE
STUDENT'S OWN NEEDS AUTOMATICALLY AND CAN THEREFORE
ADJUST THE COURSE PRESENTATION TO SUIT EACH NEW CLASS.
THAT'S THE PROFESSIONAL APPROACH TO THE TUTOR'S ROLE.

A P P E N D I X

APPENDIX   A

INTRODUCTION TO APPENDIX A

In this appendix, you will find a few ready-made explanations of the "mechanical" process (control of tongue, teeth, and lips) used to produce some of the more difficult sounds in the English language.

If more than half of the members of your class are having problems with any of these groups of sounds, drill the entire class. If only a small portion of the class has any given type of difficulty, coach them after class.

Use this information to answer questions or to coach. Time does not allow you to incorporate all this material into the eight basic sessions. Moreover, it is usually *not* needed by all students.

When tutoring, please honor the program structure of this course:

First Session: we familiarize students with the 45 or so key sounds. Their ears must be prepared before their tongues can perform accurately. "Close" is good enough for the first session. If you attempt to drill until accurate, you will probably discourage students and you will definitely lose control of time.

Second Session: we will review the sounds in the Pronunciation Key, and you may take the opportunity to correct and teach the mechanics of sound production if and when it is necessary. Their sounds should be "acceptable" in each instance; that is, not confused with any other sound. Not every student or class will have the same problem or combination of problems. Go with the flow. It is not necessary to use the extra drills on any sounds or the exercises (in either the text or Appendix) unless a problem exists.

Third Session: we work toward the perfection of the sounds already "taught".

Fourth Session and thereafter: the emphasis switches to phrases and other guides to fluency, even though we continue to strive for "perfection" in sound production as reflected in the dictionary Pronunciation Key (as defined in the Preface to this book).

DIFFICULTIES RELATED TO NATIVE LANGUAGES:

The types of problems different students have with English are related both to their individual capabilities (ear and tongue) and to the general structure of their own native languages. That is why our sign-in sheets ask for their national origin and native language(s).

While the diacritical marks used in the dictionary will probably be new to all students equally, not all languages use the Roman alphabet. Therefore, some students will be working with a relatively unfamiliar alphabet, as well as with the diacritical code marks.

For example, the Greek alphabet and Cyrillic alphabet (used in Russia, Yugoslavia and Bulgaria), use some letters similar to those used in the Roman Alphabet (used by most other European Languages, including English), but these letters are pronounced differently. Since confusion early in the class might be normal, be patient.

Many Eastern languages (Arabic, Hebrew, Chinese, Hindi, Thai, etc.) are written with characters or glyphs or cursive symbols other than our alphabet. For those students, the English (Roman) alphabet itself is one learning process, pronunciation via diacritical codes is a second, and language stress, rhythym and intonation—or melody—is a third.

Some languages are often "choppy." That is, individual syllables have equal stress. This is true of the Chinese, Japanese, and Korean languages as well as such Indo-European languages as Italian.

To teach the rhythm and melody of the English language, model a series of "la-la-la-la-la" syllables with different rhythms and tones. Everyone will laugh, but they will also get the message: they need to become aware of the phrasings and rhythms of English, its lengthening of vowels, for example. (Note the article by Allen and Haskell on stress, rhythm, and intonation, listed below.)

Because there is no way to predict which combinations of problems will occur, select only what you actually need from the following instructional materials regarding the mechanical production of sounds.

Be prepared to coach individual students after class if their problems are not typical of the class as a whole.

It is possible that, despite your very best efforts, some students will not be able to produce certain sounds consistently. Such cases might require special work. To be safe, contact a qualified speech or ESL (English as a second language) teacher. Introduce yourself and describe the problem. Ask for assistance or instruction or a referral. A specialist might wish to interview your student. If so, encourage the student to make and keep an appointment. For best results, treat the entire event as "normal" when dealing with the student.

BIBLIOGRAPHY

There are also pronunciation textbooks filled with exercises and examples which will help you to help the student recognize, produce, and descriminate among individual sounds. Here are a few:

Allen, Virginia French and John Haskell. "Teaching Intonation, Stress and Rhythm." In *Classroom Practices in Adult ESL,* ed. Ilyn and Tragardh. Washington, DC: TESOL, 1978, p. 125.

Avery, Peter and Susan Ehrlich. "The Teaching of Pronunciation: An Introduction." In *TESL Talk*, Vol. 17, No. 1. Toronto: Ontario Ministry of Culture and Immigration. (Note: this is a wonderful text, but it does not deal with the "caught/cot" contrast of some Canadian and most American dialects/varieties of English.)

Bowen, J. Donald. *Patterns of English Pronunciation.* Rowley, MA: Newbury House, 1975.

Gilbert, Judy. *Clear Speech: Pronunciation and Listening Comprehension in American English.* New York: Cambridge University Press, 1984.

Nilsen, Donald L.F. and Allene Pace Nilsen. *Pronunciation Contrasts in English.* New York: Regents, 1973.

Prator, Clifford and Betty Robinett. *Manual of American English Pronunciation,* 4th ed. New York: Holt, Rinehart & Winston, 1985.

Robinett, Betty. "The Sound System," In *Teaching English as a Second Language: Substance and Technique.* New York: McGraw-Hill, 1978, p. 64.

Trager, Edith Crowell. *The PD's in Depth.* Culver City, CA: English Language Services, 1982.

THE MECHANICS OF SOME SOUNDS

The following is a discussion—in the order in which they occur in the text in Session One—of (a) the sound production of some difficult American English sounds, (b) some notes on their occurrence in English spelling, and (c) a few exercises to practice them with:

1. THE SCHWA SOUND

The schwa is the most common vowel sound in English. It is the "uh" sound that is often heard in American speech between words and phrases when the speaker is "thinking-out-loud." (Eg., "I, uh, went to the, uh, store, uh, to get a loaf of bread"—a practice not to be encouraged in new speakers.) The schwa is a "neutral" sound made with a relaxed tongue lying in the center of the mouth. It sounds the same as the "U" with-the-arc, which the dictionary uses for stressed syllables containing the letter "U" (and occasionally the "O," "oo," or "ou" letter combinations, eg. "cut," "mud," "mother," "son," "come," "flood," "blood," "country," and "does").

The dictionary WILL use the schwa when it occurs in short "function" words when they are **un**stressed in a sentence, such as "the" and "of." (Eg., The boy had a picture **of** his mother.) Note: the nouns usually will carry the stress.

Primarily the dictionary uses the schwa to indicate unstressed "uh" sounds. Many vowels which occur in the unstressed syllable of a word will often be "reduced" to the neutral schwa sound. For example, the "A" in "above" and "about" are generally "reduced" (or written as a schwa) in the dictionary and are pronounced like the "U" of "undressed" or "up" (which the dictionary spells with the "U" with an arc.) Never mind, they sound the same. [Over cor- recters will, of course, say "ā-bove" and "ā-bout," pronouncing the "A" like its name; but in general American English we use the "uh" sound of the schwa.]

Notice the emphasized vowel in each of the following words; they are all transcribed with a schwa in the dictionary, and are pronounced "uh" as in the word "the" or "up:" "**a**bove," "ed**i**ble," "devel**o**p," "tom**a**to," "fount**ai**n," "penc**i**l," "nati**o**n," "oce**a**n," "danger**ou**s."

The schwa is also used in front of the letter "R" whenever it occurs in unstressed syllables. (Again, it will sound similar to the "U" with-the-arc that the dictionary uses for such words as "bird," "fir," "herd," "word," "urge," and "heard"—all of which are vowels in stressed syllables.) In unstressed syllables, however, the dictionary uses the schwa. For example: "moth**er**," "fath**er**," "doll**ar**," "doct**or**," "mot**or**," "col**or**," "eff**or**t," "murm**ur**," "pleas**ure**," "fut**ure**," and "theat**re**."

The schwa is also the brief and unstressed sound between the "T" and "N" in the word "button" or "eaten" and between the "T" and "L" in "bottle." The dictionary will often delete the schwa sound in these cases (they are called "syllabic consonants" in linguistics), letting the "L" or "N" stand alone as a syllable. In truth, however, the schwa or "uh" is there, however briefly.

2. THE MECHANICS OF THE "R" SOUNDS

One of the most difficult sounds in the English language is the "R". This is true because in most other languages, the "R" sound is made with the tip of the tongue **hitting** against the gum ridge (that bump behind the front teeth). A single tapping of the tongue against the gum-ridge will produce a "flap-R," as in the British pronunciation of "very" (veddy), or Spanish "pero" (but), or Japanese "sayonara" (goodbye). It is similar to the way American English generally pronounces the double-T in such words as "little," "butter," (liddle, budder) or in some single-T words such as "metal" (medal).

In some languages there is a rapid flapping (or tapping) of the tip of the tongue (usually twice) when making certain "R" sounds. These sounds are called trills, as in the Spanish "perro" (dog). The flap-R and the trill do not generally occur in standard American dialects.

The dictionary version of broadcast or standard American English does not use either the flap-R nor the trilled-R. (Neither do we use the schwa sound that the British substitute for a final "R" in such words as "fathah" (father), "deah" (dear), "mothah" (mother), etc. Some Eastern shore and Black dialects of American English use the R-less final schwa sound. You should avoid teaching it unless it is the **expected** standard pronunciation of your geographic region.

Because many students will have difficulty with this very American "R" sound, it is important to help them make it correctly even though in some cases they will continue to have difficulty discriminating between the "R" and the "L" sound. (Some languages, such as the Japanese, have the flap-R and the "L" sounds as substitutable pairs. The Japanese student, for example, will have difficulty in distinguishing between these two sounds, which in Japanese can often be substituted for each other (in most circumstances in most dialects). For example, in English, such words as butter and matter may be said with a "D" or a "T" sound in the middle without our hearing any difference in meaning. We often don't even hear the different sounds at all. This is also true in English when we say words such as "rouge," "beige" and "garage" where some use the "zh" for the final sound and others use the "J"). Yet with "metal" or "latter," a "D" sound can confuse meanings.

The retroflex-R as the American-R is called, is made by "curling" the tip of the tongue toward the gum ridge, rather than touching it (as is done by the trill and the flap-R), while the back of the tongue squeezes the throat. Therefore, the tongue retroflexes; that is, it waves, or curves up and back in the gum ridge area as the lips make a "ŭ-sound" shape—which prevents the tongue from easily reaching the gum ridge.

One way to help students say the sound correctly is to get them to produce the "ŭ" or schwa sound in front of the American-R. For example, "ŭ-red," "ŭ-right," "ŭ-read" until they get comfortable with the sound's production. The "ŭ" sound can be slowly reduced and removed while retaining that rounded lip shape necessary for the "R" production. The American-R seems to always have a slight "ŭ" or "schwa" sound in front of it, even when it occurs elsewhere in a word. Eg., "mother," "bright" (bŭr-right), "very" (ve-ŭry), etc.

Optional Review Exercise for the "R" sound with various vowels:

(TO BEGIN INSTRUCTING, THE TUTOR SAYS:)

Say "are" (ALL REPEAT) say "arm" (ALL REPEAT) Say "farm...car...her...hurt... sports...records...cry...cream."

(ALL REPEAT ALL WORDS)

You're improving. Fortunately, Americans understand the other "R's." They are not a problem in communication but they do emphasize your accent.

Because the American-R sound is voiced (with the sound coming from the back of the throat while the tongue is "curled" at the gum ridge), and because the vowel sounds that are combined with the letter "R" are formed at the front of the mouth, that combination often changes the sound of the vowel at least slightly.

As we have already learned, the dictionary often uses the tent symbol to indicate that the vowel sound is changed or modified by the "R".

```
PRINT: with 'r'
    ar = care, hair, merry
    ir = pier, fear, sheer, we're
    or = for
    ur = fur, fir, her, word, hear
schwa-r = father, dollar,
          doctor, murmur
```

Because of these changes, most of you will have difficulty hearing the right vowel sound. Just be aware that I realize these sounds might be difficult today. They will become easier as you become familiar with them during future classes.

3. VOICING REVIEW

Because voicing is so important, we should review all the voiced pairs again. Remember, the tongue and teeth are in the same position for each pair; only the voicing is added to one of them to produce the difference between them. Remember, too, that voicing means producing a vibration in the throat (larynx) of the vocal cords. This produces the voiced sound. Voicelessness occurs when this vibration is absent. Have the students practice by putting their fingers on their throat while they say the voiced "Z" sound "z-z-z-z-z-z-z". They should feel the vibration. Now, have them say the voiceless "S" sound "s-s-s-s-s-s-s". They should feel none. This contrast will be true for each of the pairs we will practice below. Get your students used to putting their fingers on their throat to feel the voicing, and get them to lengthen the sounds during their practice session, when they can.

OPTIONAL EXERCISE:

PRINT:
"th/**th**"
think/**th**ese

Say, "think...**th**ese...thought...**th**ough...north... nor**th**ern...bath...ba**th**ing." (ALL REPEAT)

ADD:
"s/z"
so/zone

Say, "so...zone...soon...zoom...hiss...his...peace... peas...facing...phasing." (ALL REPEAT)

ADD:
"sh/zh"
cash/casual

Say, "cash...casual...bush...usual...passion... pleasure...rash...rouge." (ALL REPEAT)

ADD:
"f/v"
ferry/very

Say, "ferry...very...fine...vine...after...average... offer...over...life...live...loaf...love." (ALL REPEAT)

(continue)

ADD:
"t/d"
time/dime

Say, "time...dime...trouble...double...kitten...
kidding...hotel...modal...bet...bed...coat...code.
(ALL REPEAT)

ADD:
"p/b"
pin/bin

Say, "pin...bin...pouring...boring...ripping...
ribbing...captain...cabin...cup...cub...puppy...
cabby...rip...rib." (ALL REPEAT)

ADD:
"k/g"
kilt/guilt

Say, "kilt...guilt...cut...gut...backer...bagger...
uncle...ugly...ache...egg...back...bag."
(ALL REPEAT)

ADD:
"ch/j"
choose/juice

Say, "choose...juice...cherry...Jerry...itching...
edging...a chest...adjust...itch...edge...match...
Madge...magic...major." (ALL REPEAT)

NOTE: REPEAT ANY OR ALL PAIRS UNTIL THE SOUNDS ARE FAIRLY ACCURATE. DO NOT EXPECT PERFECTION, BUT WHEN IT HAPPENS, BE SURE TO SAY SO. COMPLIMENTS ARE USEFUL AS BOTH FEEDBACK AND INCENTIVE.

THERE ARE MANY EXAMPLES OF PAIRS OF WORDS FOR USE IN THESE KINDS OF DRILLS WHICH CAN BE FOUND IN PRONUNCIATION TEXTBOOKS. HOWEVER, THE EXERCISES PROVIDED IN THIS TEXT HAVE PROVED ADEQUATE.

4. THE MECHANICS OF THE SYBILANT GROUP ("S" FAMILY)

(SEE ALSO EXERCISE 3 ON VOICING AND EXERCISE 7 [APPENDIX "B"] ON THE ADDING OF "S" TO NOUNS AND VERBS IN ENGLISH)

Sibilants are made with a groove down the middle of the tongue over which the air flows. Sibilants are sounds that can be said to have a "hissing" quality.

(1) The "S" and "Z" are made with the tip of the tongue making a groove near the gum ridge. (2) The "sh" and "zh" are made with the tongue grooved and pulled back behind the gum ridge. (3) The "ch" and "J" are made by flattening the sides of the grooved tongue against the sides of the gum ridge (or teeth) and slightly exploding the sound, as we do with the other "explosive" sounds such as the "J" and "D".

Many linguists feel that the "ch" is a "T" rapidly followed by the "sh" and that the "J" is a "D" rapidly followed by a "zh" sound. No matter, they are common in English and fairly easy sounds to make.

The "zh" is the most problematic since it seldom occurs at the beginning of words. Words borrowed from the French, such as "genre", are pronounced with a "zh" at the beginning by some speakers; and, of course, some pronounce Ms. Gabor's name, Zsa Zsa, with the "zh" sound at the beginning. It is more likely however that American speakers, at least occasionally, will substitute a "J" sound for the "zh" when it occurs at the beginning of a word or at the end of words borrowed from the French, such as "rouge", "beige" and "garage". The "zh" does occur fairly naturally, however, in such words as "pleasure", "leisure" and "azure" because the "Z" sound followed by the "yōō (or ū)" sound produces a "zh".

This rule also accounts for the unusual spelling combinations in which the "ch" and "J" sounds occur. When a "T" is followed by a "yōō" sound, one will automatically get, in rapid speech, a "ch" sound. Eg., "temperature", "literature", "virtue" and "don't you." When the "D" sound is followed immediately by the "yōō" sound, you often produce a "J". Eg., "education", "modulate" and "did you". Note: the British or Canadian speaker may even get a "J" in such words as "Tuesday" or "tune" (which in slow speech are pronounced "tyūz-day" and "tyūne") as opposed to the American pronunciation of "tōōz-day" and "tōōn."

5. THE VOICED AND VOICELESS "TH"

The "TH" in English has both a voiced and voiceless sound. (Note Exercise 3 above on the other voiced and voiceless pairs of consonants in English.)

The "TH" sounds are made by putting the tip of the tongue between the teeth and letting the air flow across the flat of the tongue. (Note: In rapid speech we sometimes let the tongue slip slightly back and press against the back of the teeth.) Get your students to hold a finger against their lips (as in saying "be quiet") and as they say a "th," their tongue should touch their finger.

The "TH" sound occurs in few other languages, and so it is usually substituted with the "T" or "D" by most second language learners (or as the French do, with the "S" or "Z"). Some native speakers of English do this also.

The more difficult problem for these sounds is not production but discriminating between the voiced and voiceless "TH." Fortunately, the context in which most words occur will not hinder understanding even if other sounds are substituted; but if the student wants to practice these sounds there are many words in English to draw on for exercises.

To distinguish between the voiced and voiceless "TH," the student will have to lengthen the "TH" sound sufficiently to notice if there is voicing (making a vibration in the throat) or not. For example, if the student says 'th-th-th-th-ink", (lengthening the first sound) one can tell that there is no voicing at the beginning of the word, as opposed to saying "th-th-th-th-ey", where voicing occurs from the beginning to the end.

Here are some words to practice with:

Voiced: the, they, them, there, those, that, father, mother, either, northern, bathing, other, bathe, loathe, either, though

Voiceless: think, thin, thirty, thousand, three, thought, ether, anther, author, south, north, math, bath, teeth, fifth, sixteenth

6. THE MECHANICS OF THE "ENG" SOUND

The "eng" sound in English is a nasalized sound (like the "M" and "N") made in the back of the mouth like the "K" and "G" sounds. In fact, the "eng" occurs naturally when the letter "N" is followed by a "K" or "G", as in such words as "think", "uncle", "banquet", "sing", "length", "hunger", "longer" and "tango". Unfortunately, most second language speakers want to say the "G" sound (and, even, occasionally a "K" sound) in addition to the "eng" whenever they see the "N" followed by a "G". This is the accurate pronunciation for such words as "hunger", "longer", "tango", "linger", "finger", "angle", "single", "longest", etc. It is NOT true for the bulk of "n+g" situations which occur in English, such as "sing", "hanger", "lung", "singing", "longed", "changing" (note the "J" sound for the first "n+g" combination), "wrong", etc.

Note, too, that when the "N" is followed by the "K" or "G" the "eng" occurs if this combination is in the same syllable. If the "n" occurs at the end of one syllable, and the "K" or "G" occur at the beginning of the next syllable or word, then the "eng" will only seem to occur in rapid speech. Note, for example, such words as "unkind", "pancake", "on guard", "ingrate", etc. When these words are spoken rapidly, native speakers automatically produce a nasalized "eng"; but when said slowly, a clear "N" sound can be produced without any "eng".

OPTIONAL EXERCISE: (for practice with "n" + "k")

PRINT: "ng" sound ng + k = "eng" +k

For example, when words are spelled with the "N" followed by the "K" we pronounce both the "eng" and the "K". The dictionary will show the "ng" symbol and the "K" symbol.

ADD: ink = ingk think = thingk

Say, "ink...think...pink...drink." (ALL REPEAT)

ADD: think/thinking drink/drinking

Say, "think/thinking...drink/drinking."
Remember to say the "K" but not the "G" sound. (And no "K" sound at the **end** of these words.) (ALL REPEAT)

ADD: think/thinker drink/drinker

Say, "think/thinker...drink/drinker." Remember to say the "eng" and the "K" sound in these words.

APPENDIX B

INTRODUCTION TO APPENDIX B

Of course grammar is essential to the mastery of the English language; so the few points of grammar for the narrower focus of this course are already presented in script and notes.

This course cannot—and does not claim to—teach grammar. Because all the class periods are full as scripted, you will not have the spare time needed to cover grammar even if you are capable of teaching it.

Use this information to answer questions or to coach. Only if you add an extra session for grammar or job-specific vocabulary should you present this material in full...time does not allow it, otherwise.

If you have students whose grammar is a handicap **despite** improved pronunciation, be prepared to give them information regarding appropriate classes in nearby schools. Many high schools and community colleges are offering classes for General Education Diploma (GED), or in Adult Basic Education (ABE) or Adult Continuing Education (ACE).

Among the rules of grammar presented in this book and in this Appendix are those relating to both prepositional phrases and plural forms.

Prepositional phrases and other indicators of phrasing-for-sense are fully discussed in the script, with exercises provided.

Extensive information is given below regarding the formation of plurals because abridged dictionaries usually enter only the singular form of the given word. Therefore students must be prepared (a) to recognize—as well as pronounce —the listed form if the plural is found in reading materials; and (b) to be able to form regular plurals, since these do not appear in most abridged dictionaries; and (c) to recognize the irregular plurals that are listed at the end of the word definition for certain entries.

Note that the rules for the pronunciation of the "S" (plural) added to nouns and the "S" (third person singular) added to verbs are the same.

7. ADDING AN "S" TO NOUNS AND VERBS

Plural forms of most nouns and the third person singular of verbs are indicated by adding an "S" to the final syllable of the word. But the final "S" sometimes has an "S" sound and sometimes a "Z" sound.
(To begin instructing, the Tutor says:) The dictionary shows only the irregular endings. Regular endings are not printed.

```
PRINT:
regular/irregular
```

Fortunately there are some rules to help:

```
PRINT:
Formula for Regular Plurals and
Third Person Singular of Verbs:
—If the word ends in a voiced
   sound, consonant or vowel,
   except for sibilants, add "s"
   and say "z".
```

Examples: bug/bugs, fade/fades, ski/skis, plow/plows.
(ALL REPEAT)

```
ADD:
—If the word ends in an
   unvoiced sound, except for
   sibilants, add "s" and say "s".
```

Examples: hit/hits, kite/kites.

```
ADD:
—If the word ends with "S
   Family," sounds (sibilants),
   add "s" (or "es") and
   pronounce as a new syllable,
   "-ez."
```

Examples: church/churches, kiss/kisses, wash/washes, judge/judges, etc.

All endings consistent with this formula are considered "regular" and are not shown in the dictionary.

> PRINT:
> Formula for Some Irregular
> uses of the "s" for plural or
> Third Person Singular:
> —Certain words ending in "o"
>   add "es" and are pronounced
>   "z"

Examples: tomato/tomatoes, go/goes

> ADD:
> —Words ending in "f" change
>   to "v" and add "s"
>   pronounced as "z"

Examples: wife/wives, half/halves.

> ADD:
> —Certain words ending in "y"
>   change the "y" to "i" and
>   add "es" pronounced "z"

Examples: cry/cries, try/tries (but note: buy/buys, ferry/ferrys).

The unabridged dictionary prints only the irregular endings, which you will find at the end of the definition for the given word.

There is no easy answer to plural forms. Even native speakers of English have difficulty with these endings. When in doubt, especially if you are writing, check an unabridged dictionary.

However, in spoken English, the production of the differences in sound for all the "S" endings are almost automatic. The rules have been made according to the **easiest way to say** the pluralized or third person singular word. Therefore, these particular rules are more important in writing than in speaking. Whatever you say, you will be understood.

Optional Exercises Using The Formula for Plurals:

> PRINT:
> books
> parts
> tops

The voiceless "S" sound is used if the plural occurs after a voiceless consonant. Remember the voiced and voiceless pairs of sounds we have just learned? Say, "books...parts...tops." (ALL REPEAT)

(continue)

PRINT: "z" sound
tree/trees
see/sees
toe/toes
day/days
say/says

The voiced "Z" sound is used when the word ends with one of our six vowel letters (A, E, I, O, U, or Y) or a voiced consonant.
Say, "trees...sees...toes...days...says" (ALL REPEAT)

ADD: "z" sound
bills
hams
runs
jars

Say, "bills...hams...runs...jars." (ALL REPEAT)
Remember, that some words end in a vowel sound but may end with a silent consonant, such as a "W".

ADD: "z" sound
cows
flows
blahs
coups

Say, "cows...flows...blahs...coups."

ADD: change "y" to "i", add "es" = "z"
fly/flies
try/tries
story/stories
carry/carries

Some words that end in "Y" are spelled with an "ies" for the plural. You will have to learn these words as they occur.
Say, "flies...tries...stories...carries."

(continue)

```
ADD: "es" = "z"
sound
potato-es
tomato-es
go-goes
```

Some words ending in a vowel form the plural or third person singular by adding "es." In this case we do not add a syllable, but we do pronounce the "Z" sound.

Say, "potatoes...tomatoes...goes." (ALL REPEAT)

There is an exception to these rules when the noun or the verb ends in an "S" or "Z" sound. This is also true if they end with any of the other "hissing" sounds we have learned (the "ch", "sh", "zh," or "J"). In these cases an extra syllable is added to the word. It is written "es" and pronounced "ez."

```
PRINT:
bus = busses
kiss = kisses
buzz = buzzes
wash = washes
church = churches
```

Can you hear the added syllable? Say, "bus/busses." (ALL REPEAT) Say, kiss/kisses...buzz/buzzes... wash/washes...church/churches...(REPEAT ALL PAIRS.)

```
ADD:
garage/garages
judge/judges
```

Remember that the letter "J" seldom occurs at the end of a word in English but the letter "G" often sounds like the "J". Say, "garage/garages...judge/judges."

Remember, too, that the letter "X" is pronounced like a "ks" at the end of a word in English and the letter "C" often sounds like an "S". Say, "tax/taxes... place/places."

```
PRINT:
write/writes
hide/hides
use/uses
```

Always check your dictionary. Be careful of those words that end in the "silent-E," as in words like "hide (hidez)...write (writes)...and use (use-ez)." (POINT TO THESE WORDS). Say, "write/writes...hide/hides... use/uses (ALL REPEAT.)

Optional Exercise:

NOTE: WHEN WE ADD AN "S" TO WORDS ENDING IN
THE SILENT-E WE MUST IGNORE THE "E" AND LOOK
FOR THE FINAL SOUND IN THE WORD. IS IT VOICED
OR NOT? FOR EXAMPLE, IN THE WORD "WRITE" THE
FINAL SOUND IS A "T," AND YOU ADD THE "S" SOUND;
IN "HIDE" IT IS A "D" AND YOU ADD THE "Z" SOUND;
IN THE VERB "TO USE" IT IS A "Z" AND YOU WOULD
ALSO ADD A "Z" SOUND. (NOTE, TOO THAT THE NOUN
"THE USE" CAN ALSO BE PRONOUNCED WITH A FINAL
"S" SOUND.)

OPTION:
(IF YOU HAVE TIME ASK THE STUDENTS FOR OTHER
WORDS, NOUNS AND VERBS, THEY KNOW THAT END
WITH A SILENT-E AND HAVE THEM TRY TO ADD THE
CORRECT "S" SOUND.)

ADDITIONAL OPTIONAL INFORMATION:

```
PRINT:
PLACE/PLACES
```

WHAT WOULD YOU DO TO A WORD SUCH AS "PLACE?"
WHAT IS THE SOUND THAT ENDS THIS WORD?
THAT'S RIGHT, NOT THE "E" BUT THE LETTER "C"
WHICH IS PRONOUNCED LIKE AN "S". So
WE ADD THE SYLLABLE "ES" BUT SAY "EZ"
Say, "PLACE/PLACES."

Now let's see how our dictionary treats these individual cases.

The addition of the letter "S" to form the plural of a noun is considered a "regular" plural. Therefore, our dictionary does not show a separate entry or spelling. This is true of the "S" added to verbs, also.

NOTE: MAKE SURE THAT STUDENTS KNOW THAT
THE "S" ADDED TO VERBS IS NOT A PLURAL BUT A
MARKER FOR THE THIRD PERSON SINGULAR FORM
OF THE PRESENT TENSE VERB, ACCOMPANIED
WITH "HE, SHE, IT", AND NAMES, FOR EXAMPLE.

Similarly, the "es" ending is considered a regular ending for words which end in the "s/z/j/sh/ch" or "zh" sounds and it is not always shown in the dictionary.

Finally, for some words that end in "F" sounds, the "regular" plural rule would call for an "S" ending. However, that combination sound is difficult to say.

Therefore, we change the "F" to its voiced-pair partner, "V", and add the voiced plural, "Z".

> PRINT:
> "f" endings become
> "v + s"
>   self/selves
>   knife/knives
>   half/halves
>   wife/wives

As you use these (and all other) plurals, you will soon be able to apply the correct sounds without even thinking about it.

PRACTICAL WORD POWER

Course Grading Form (suggested)

Starting date: _____

Completion date: _____

Tutor: _____

Employer/sponsor: _____

Report to: _____

STUDENT'S NAME	Social Sec. #	Language & Nationality	Class sessions (overall)								Newspaper Tests	Dictionary Test/Final	Notes & Comments
			1	2	3	4	5	6	7	8			

Guidelines for grading by letter or number:

At or near perfection.........."A" or 10 & 9

Slight variation, immaterial......."B" or 8-7

Obvious variation; understandable "C" or 6-4

Occasionally unclear............"D" or 3-2

Grading by broad category:

S = Satisfactory; at or above class norm

I = Inadequate; below class norm

U = Unsatisfactory; no progress

NOTE: Because it is impossible to grade up to ten students on over forty-five sounds each, use the "S-I-U" system for all eight overall sessions, but give letter or number grades to all individual newspaper article recitations and the final test.

TOPICAL INDEX

Printed in the United States
1150700001B/153